Creating Connections

In Ericksonian Approaches To
Hypnosis And Therapy
Volume 1

ISBN: 0995358109

ISBN-13: 978-0-9953581-0-2

Creating Connections: In Ericksonian Approaches To Hypnosis And Therapy/ Rob McNeilly Volume 1

Tandava Press
www.tandavapress.com
tandavapress@gmail.com

Printed in the United States of America

This book is offered as a humble gesture of appreciation of the continuation of Milton Erickson's heritage into the future.

Contents

Foreword: Bill O'Hanlon   vii

Addictions: A Solution Oriented Guide   1

An Ericksonian Approach To Sleep Problems Waking Up To
Individual Approaches   13

A Place To Learn In - A Place To Teach From   23

Stopping Smoking: Does It Have To Be Difficult?   37

Creating A Context For Therapy: Is There Anything Else?   43

The Emerging Language Of Emotions And The Body   54

Ethics – An Evolution   61

Hypnosis, Dissociation And Spontaneous Trance:

Erickson's Contribution   67

Learning To Learn   74

Psychotherapy In The Drift Of Social History Time,

Pace And Power   88

About Nothing   93

The Empathy Dilemma   103

After Trauma – Healing The Mind Body And Soul   109

About The Author   123

Foreword: Bill O'Hanlon

The Context Called Rob McNeilly

I met Rob years ago after we were both students of the now late psychiatrist and hypnotherapist Milton H. Erickson.

We not only became friends but quickly realised we were simpatico in our therapeutic ideas and approaches.

Rob is a possibility-oriented fellow, in life and in his approach to psychotherapy and change.

Rob was trained in medicine, with all that entails, both the rigorous and challenging academic and scientific knowledge he had to master, and the tendency to see people as problems and pathology.

But somewhere along the line, this pathologising approach began to wear thin for Rob and his natural optimism and belief in people's abilities and resources began to re-emerge.

Along with the influence of the ideas of Dr. Erickson, Rob and I share a background in being influenced by EST, The Landmark Forum, and the work of Fernando Flores.

These approaches show in Rob's interest in how contexts influence mood and perception.

The papers and pieces included here show that constant playful openness and questioning, that shifting of contexts from certainty to curiosity.

That is one of the things I consistently appreciate about Rob: his gentle sense of humour and playfulness. He doesn't take himself too seriously, although he is serious about contributing to others and to the fields of change, hypnosis and coaching.

Reading this book invites you to live in the questions and be curious. There are answers here, yes, and solutions, but more than those bits of wisdom is a playful invitation to be a lifelong learner, to be curious, to not know, and to find out together.

It promises to be a fun and fruitful journey. Turn the page and follow the paths (or wander off, if you'd like – it's surely okay with Rob).

Yours in possibilities,

Bill O'Hanlon
Santa Fe, New Mexico, 2014

Addictions: A Solution Oriented Guide

Introduction:

We live in a disconnected society. Even without the Internet, computers, mobile phones, SMS there are increasing signs of disconnection from our families, our body, and our soul from experience itself. There is a crisis of purpose and meaning, most evident in our youth who are wondering is it worth the effort, and middle class middle aged individuals questioning whether it's worth maintaining the effort.

With all this disconnection and crisis of meaning, it's not surprising that people are looking for something consistent, and also something to fill the painfully empty space ... drugs, alcohol, gambling, sex ... the list is as long as humans are inventive. The dilemma comes when the attempt to fill the gap, escape the pain, deal with the suffering, leads to further pain and suffering which then invites further escape, and the escalation continues.

There is a massive amount of suffering resulting – personal, relational, social, economic, and in spite of the best intentions to restrict and control these activities they are increasing, and there doesn't appear to be a satisfactory solution so far.

I find it helpful to remind myself that we are never dealing with addiction; we are always dealing with a person. This allows me to question what addiction is for this individual. Erickson reminded us repeatedly that each client is an individual, and we need to tailor our approach to the individual rather than requiring them to fit our theories and protocols. Instead of assuming that we as experts hold the key to a client's solution, we can wonder with each individual client about their individual experience. By asking what aspect of ... is still troubling them, is still active for them, is still disturbing them, we have an opportunity to more closely explore what is likely to be required by them to deal with whatever aspect required to let them get on with their life.

There is such a variety of individual responses that while it's appealing to think that there might be a single unifying approach such an idea then seems unhelpful to any individual client.

The everyday understanding of addictions is that they are beyond our control, so we find ourselves in the grip of some chemically induced craving which we are taken over by, and which we might be able to resist for a time with the use of supreme will power, and even then the addiction will probably win. The process is expected to be accompanied by severe withdrawal symptoms and much suffering. Part of the "QUIT" literature states that nicotine addiction is even stronger than heroin, and I can't help wondering how unhelpful this comment might be! Once an addict, always an addict, and there is even talk of addictive personalities applied to people who get over one addiction, only to fall prey to another. Conquering gambling was followed by a drinking problem, and when that was defeated, overeating took its place.

This understanding of addictions overlooks the human, social, and in particular the linguistic components.

Farmers in the hills of Malaysia have for centuries smoked opium at the end of a long harvest, a hard journey, a special occasion, and then the pipe is packed away for months or years, with no problems. In a recent TV documentary, heroin addicts in Moscow were shown handcuffed to a bed after stopping the heroin, with the knowledge that there was no possibility of access to the drug, and there were no signs of withdrawal.

These are merely two examples where the sudden withdrawal was not followed by any adverse reaction, and must have us wonder what's happening when there are withdrawal effects, sometimes very severe.

I claim that an addiction exists, as a legitimate experience, and is created in language, in a social environment which sets up specific expectations, and although we can comfortably and usefully use the word, we will want to be aware ourselves of the changeable nature of the addiction. Addiction is a label that has a use, but has no solid existence outside language. This is a cornerstone of the solution oriented approach, and is one of its greatest contributions to the process of change.

Erickson sent a man with a life-threatening drinking problem to the Phoenix Botanical Gardens to contemplate the wide variety of cactus plans there that could go for years without a drink. He reports that this experience gave the man the hint he needed to make the permanent change.

A woman wanted help from me years ago because of what she called her pethidine addiction. She was using way more than the prescribed dose for her chronic kidney pain, which was about to be surgically corrected, precipitating her crisis of panicking about having withdrawal symptoms in hospital, leading to the uncovering of her shady efforts to maintain her pethidine supply over the years. I warned her that she could expect a horrific weekend, and exaggerated the likely bodily responses to the sudden absence of the drug. She left rather pale, in anticipation of a weekend from hell. She rang on the Monday, and asked when the symptoms would begin, and was shocked and relieved to hear that that had already finished. Because she was expecting the worst, any sensations she notice were discounted as insignificant, and let pass without note. Her problem was over before it began, to everyone's relief.

When we look for strengths and resourcefulness in our clients, we can help them to reconnect with these with carefully crafted questions. Some people just don't need to explore the traumas and pains of the past to complete them and move on. Many are relieved to discover that they don't necessarily have to go into the angst of it all to heal. Milton Erickson was a major explorer of this important territory, and Steve de Shazer, and Bill O'Hanlon have further added to the conversation. I have tried to add texture to the field by introducing the action aspect of moods and emotions as well as the body as a store of moods, whether helpful or not.

Traditionally we have asked questions to explore what's happening for a client so we can make a diagnosis, design a treatment plan, which we can then begin to implement and manage. If instead, we ask questions to lead in the direction of what might be missing for any individual, we can then explore, with the client's active participation, what they might be overlooking, or might want to look for. This creates a very different mood in the therapeutic conversation, and is likely to be more satisfying for all.

In the solution oriented approach, we find it more useful to assume that so called addictions are patterns of behaviour which, since they began, can also stop. Either of these changes, we assume, do not have to be caused by anything in particular. If an unwanted behaviour has been learnt, it can be unlearnt, and a new, different, more acceptable one can be learnt in its place.

From this starting point, we can explore what is happening when the addiction is less pressing, or not noticed at all. What was the person doing before the addiction became part of their life? What will be different when they have left it behind and moved on? Who will be the first to know? These presupposi-tional questions are so helpful in helping to make the future more real and attainable as a result.

Counselling Contributions

If we ask a client about how they have dealt with similar situation in the past, what changes they may have noticed since deciding to make an appointment, they might discover some resources that had passed unnoticed and by noticing them, have a more ready access to these resources.

If we ask about times when the problem isn't so acute, is less pressing, or perhaps not there at all, this can further shift the direction towards what they can then do to have more of those experiences, and less of the unwanted ones.

If we ask about what they are anticipating will be different when they are OK again, when they have completed their therapy with us, and perhaps even if a miracle happened and they discovered that they were OK, we can explore the possibility of being OK, and sometimes this breaks the heavy grip of resignation when they had given up hope of ever getting past the unwanted experience.

If a client has been suffering for any significant length of time, the problem can assume a life of its own, and we are then faced with the dilemma of trying to connect a client with their solution when they are waiting for some external agent to change – the weather, the economy, government policies – a change which at least most of us won't have much influence over. Waiting for a solution to arrive from a place where it won't come from will be a long and frustrating process for everyone. Steve de Shazer labels people who present this way as *complainants*, and recommends acknowledging their pain and suffering, complimenting them on their strength and forbearance, and then asking about some small change that they themselves may be able to initiate. This will sometimes allow some movement when previous attempts failed.

Other people are sent by well meaning others, some of whom may be therapist and will tell us that so and so thought that we could help – an indication that we may be talking with a de Shazer *visitor*. He recommends that here we join with their disinterest or annoyance at having to see us, and explore what the least change might be that the sender would accept to stop sending them. Sometimes some small change can be initiated, which can snowball into something acceptable to client, sender, and us.

Problems can be thought of as a series of actions, often rigidly choreographed and when the sequence is interrupted, there can be a disruption to the integrity of the problem, sometimes leading to its dissolving. By identifying what actions are already being taken that are helpful, we can encourage the client to do them more. By identifying what actions are unhelpful, we can encourage the client to do them less. By altering the sequence of the steps in the doing of the problem, by omitting some steps or even adding others, the pattern of behaviours can be disrupted in a helpful way. Giving unspecified tasks can give the flexibility for a client to do what they need to do to let the old sequence go, and a more useful sequence to begin to form.

Encouraging a client to refrain from changing until more information is gathered, until a parent or partner is ready, until the client is more certain that they are ready ... these constraints can have a helpfully disruptive influence on the problem, while linking the experience of the problem to some onerous activity can put the client off, and they might avoid the problem to avoid the ordeal.

Whenever a client brings a problem to us, we can look to find what concern is giving the necessity for that client. What concern does this client have that has the situation be experienced as a problem, that someone without this concern might not consider it a problem, or not worth attending to? If we can identify this concern, either speculatively or in conversation with the client, articulating this concern has the predictable result of massively expanding the self appreciation of the client. Sometimes this is sufficient for them to say that they now don't require Counselling. The experience transforms from a circumstance which negates the integrity of the sufferer into one where the client feels worthwhile *because* they have the problem!

Hypnotic Contributions
If we begin with the assumption that hypnosis is an experience involving the focusing of attention leading to increased absorption in that experience, we can usefully explore what unhelpful focusing of attention is contributing to the creation and maintenance of the problem, and what alternative direction

of mode of focusing of attention may be useful, helpful, or relevant.

If we ask what ways of attending to their circumstances are helping to create or maintain a problem, we can observe opportunities to interact which otherwise might not appear. Is the client overly associated with some aspect of their experience? Is there some other experience that they would be better off associating with, attending to instead of avoiding?

Our observations about hypnotic experience give us an additional viewpoint here. In any addiction, there is a focus on or association with the addictive behaviour – gambling, alcohol, whatever, and a focusing away or dissociation from whatever else is happening. This can alert us to exploring what emotion, action, experience the person may be avoiding (focusing away or dissociating from) and we can then assist them to address this issue, if it is helpful.

An ambitious self employed insurance salesman was happily married, with a young child, and had increasing guilt and shame over his inability to stop visiting massage parlours. A child from a previous marriage had died under tragic circumstances in Europe, and he had never faced his pain from leaving that marriage, and not taken care of his child. He was plagued by worries that maybe if he had stayed in that marriage, the child would still be alive, but the thoughts were so painful that he would visit a massage parlour to relieve the pain. When he stopped avoiding the grief, and dealt with his loss and the reality of the situation, recognising that his mere presence would not have guaranteed anything, and may have even made things worse, he visibly relaxed, and lost interest in the activities which had been threatening to take over his life and destroy it. The seemingly massive problem disappeared like a burst bubble, into nothing, and the only withdrawal symptom he experienced was relief.

It can also be useful to wonder how the client may be "hypnotised" by the problem, and find ways for them to avoid this.

Because addictive behaviour has a hypnotic quality – time distortion, dissociation, automatic behaviour – assisting someone to "not be hypnotised" by the gambling or whatever can be helpful. Addicts report consistently that they feel taken over, that another entity moves in and takes control, and it is as if they are a powerless bystander, condemned to merely sit back and watch as the worst happens. There is also reports of a dream-like quality of their experience – a fuzziness, or a terrible clarity – which have commonalities with dreams and trance.

A young woman was struggling with her addiction to cheese. She couldn't keep cheese in the house without eating every crumb, and would even get out of bed in the middle of the night and buy cheese from an all night store, bring it home and demolish it. I asked her to visit the local supermarket, and stand in front of the cheese section, to see how the cheese would try its hardest to force her to reach out and buy it, and to see how easy it could be for her to keep her hands comfortably by her sides, and walk away with a peaceful satisfied feeling. She reported that after standing in front of the cheese, she went and stood in front of the sweets, with equal satisfaction, and equally comfortably still hands.

A man in his forties wanted hypnosis to help stop smoking cigarettes. They helped him to relax, he said, but the smell was becoming unacceptable, and his general fitness was suffering. His wife and children were nagging him, for his own sake, they said, but this seemed to get in the way of him stopping. If he stopped, would he be giving in to their requirements, and go against his strongly independent way of being. In hypnosis I reminded him that the cigarettes had been nagging him to smoke them, and had interfered with his independent right to breathe fresh air. His independence helped to detach (dissociate) him from the smoking, and he had a sense of achievement at being free from the "hypnotic" influence of the cigarettes.

Other Considerations

A colleague asks clients "What problem may this be a solution to?" And opens a different line of interactions that had been previously overlooked. Some unwanted experienced can be thought of as the body or the world attempting to help. I like to remind clients that a petrol gauge showing nearly empty might be a nuisance, but it would be a greater problem if it didn't happen!

A woman couldn't stop herself going to the casino, even though she was spending the money she worked hard to earn, and was saving to take herself and her family to her dream place (USA). She had a harsh upbringing and found it difficult to do anything just for herself and any attempt was accompanied by guilt. She readily recognised that pleasing herself was something she had never learnt, and that although the gambling was something that was just for her, she would be willing to learn other, more acceptable ways of doing something just for her. She could enjoy reading a book in the bath, a second cup of coffee over lunch, a facial. She thought it would be her husband who would be most surprised, and her young daughter most relieved. She herself turned out to be the one who was most appreciative.

In conclusion, let's always remember that addictions, like all human experiences are created in language, are individually experienced, have a strong emotional aspect, a body learning component, and so are open to influence through the individual experiences of learning.

An Ericksonian Approach To Sleep Problems Waking Up To Individual Approaches

Abstract

Instead of trying for a diagnosis of the cause of the sleeping problem and treating that, there is a place for asking "What's missing for this individual?" And begin to look with that person to assist them to find it, so normality can return. Two distinct categories are outlined, and corresponding clinical approaches are discussed. A case is made to go beyond some simplistic formula, to offer more than relaxation, so the individuality of each client can be respected, and the approach tailored to that individual.

Cases are presented from the work of Milton H Erickson, and from my own practice to illustrate the use of this approach clinically.

Introduction

I first met Milton Erickson in 1977 and became an instant admirer. I was taken by his novel approach, his light mood and his dogged attention to detail that would be helpful. At the same time, I joined the long line of people who were mystified by the man and his work. What he was doing was obviously effective, but what, exactly was he doing? There didn't seem to be any logic to his methods, although there was a sense of some pattern which seemed so obvious to him, and so frustratingly elusive to me and others.

Some light began to appear when I stopped trying to understand his reasons according to some overarching theory, and began to appreciate his attention to observing minute detail to make use of in THIS session with THIS person. It seems obvious now, but at the time, nearly 40 years ago, that he was not interested in applying some preexisting theory, and totally focused on exploring the individual experience of whoever he was working with. Coming from a medical background, where information gathering was designed to make a diagnosis, formulate a treatment plan, so that treatment could begin, Erickson's approach of gathering information about THIS person to begin to interact with THIS person felt like a foreign language, or maybe even alien.

"Each person is an individual. Hence, psychotherapy should be formulated to meet the uniqueness of the individual's needs, rather than tailoring the person to fit the Procrustean bed of a hypothetical theory of human behaviour" Milton H Erickson, M.D.[1]

Erickson's insistence on tailoring the treatment to the client, which was so radical when he first articulated it, has become main-stream, like so many radical principles.

As an abstraction of following some of his principles and teaching them over the last 30 years, I have also found it useful to replace the question "What's wrong, that needs fixing?" With "What's missing, that we can explore?" "When a client comes to see you, they bring their own solution, only they don't know that they bring their solution, so have a very nice time, looking with the client, to help them find their own solution that they didn't know that they brought into the therapy session.[2]"

I like to ask each client about their likes, as this shifts the mood to one of optimism, and pleasure, as well as providing an opportunity to explore these activities for evidence of the missing resource which is resulting in them having the problem that they have.

I find that following these principles, I am conversing with another human being, rather than a case; about a resource which has been lost, misplaced, or become dusty or rusty from lack of use, rather than with pathology; with a potentially whole and healthy individual who has lost their way, rather than a patient suffering from a condition. I much prefer this way of working, and clients and student all seem to prefer it also.

Following an Ericksonian approach, then, adds an interesting dimension to writing about a group of experiences like sleep problems, since they will occur individually in very different individuals each with their unique response and responsiveness. Nevertheless there are some general observations we can investigate, and some individual examples can be shared, so the reader can make their own connections and corrections. Also whatever method of dealing with problems, attention to Erickson's principles can add effectiveness and satisfaction.[3]

We experience going to sleep as a natural, spontaneous event, and so if we *try* to go to sleep, we set up a bind like *trying to be spontaneous*. To help break this cycle of becoming wakeful by *trying* to sleep, we will be most effective if we can identify what a client is already doing, so we can at least avoiding doing more of that, and perhaps assist the client to succeed by doing the opposite. By assuming that the client has somehow got stuck in the problem, we can explore ways to help them get unstuck again, and return to their natural experience without needing to have a detailed explanation of the problem which has then disappeared.

In a world after Einstein, we can no longer talk about cause and effect, since sometimes causes are caused by the cause, or even by the effect for example, if someone is worrying about a problem at work and is losing sleep, is it the worrying about the problem at work that causes the sleep disturbance, or the lack of sleep that adds to the worry? Perhaps we can cut the Gordian knot, and avoid the time-consuming quest for an overarching understanding of how to untangle the situation, and begin to explore the individual idiosyncratic experience of each idiosyncratic individual client.

Sometimes dealing with the problem allows sleep to return, and sometime there is a poor sleep habit that remains. Sometimes dealing with the sleeping trouble allows for a resolution of the problem, or then allows for the problem to be dealt with. As long as we are dealing with these mysterious creatures called human beings, it seems useful to remain uncertain about which will be the best way to proceed, and be willing to be open to their influence.

A man consulted Erickson, stating that he had only managed 2 hours sleep for several years, and asked for help. Erickson guaranteed a cure provided he would be willing to give up 8 hours of sleep. The man willingly agreed since he had been losing nearly that amount of sleep every night for years. Erickson had discovered that the client hated polishing the wooden floors of his house, so he could instruct the man to wait until bed-time, and instead of going to bed, he could polish the floor until the usual getting up time. He could then get ready for a day's work. He would only have lost 2 hours sleep. On the fourth night the man informed his son that he was going to lie down for a minute to rest his eyes. He woke up 8 hours later. Erickson insisted that he keep a bottle of floor polish by his bed and any time he had difficulty going to sleep, he could polish the floor all night long. Erickson reported that the man had not missed a night's sleep since.

When someone says they have a sleeping difficulty, I always ask them what they hate doing most, and listen for something that can be done at night (like balancing their cheque account, or ironing a shirt) in case it might be helpful.

Method

When I ask a client with sleep difficulties "What's missing?" the responses fall into the categories of difficulties *going* to sleep and difficulties *staying* asleep. Because the problems are experienced very differently, the approaches need to be correspondingly different to meet the individual's needs.

Difficulties Going To Sleep

Difficulties can include tension, an overactive mind, worrying, physical discomfort or pain, and tiredness without sleepiness.

If the concern is *tension,* then *relaxation* is likely to be what's missing, and we can expect to be able to assist such a client by asking them to *"Close your eyes, let your body relax, and let your mind drift to some pleasing, relaxing scene – past or present, real or imagined, in any way that is pleasing and useful to you."* This situation is one of the few instances where a standard relaxation approach is helpful, in my experience.

If the problem is stated to be *an overactive mind,* then some learning involving *slowing down of mental functioning* will be relevant. We can invite such an individual to *"Take your own, slow time to attend to what I'm saying, to become disinterested in my voice or any other external noises, and even to your own internal thoughts, as you enjoy the effortless experience of letting everything slow down so you can feel more peaceful, more at ease, more aware of how you want to be, how you really are."*

When a client complains that they are kept awake by *worrying,* what's likely to be learning how to *not worry.* We can invite them to *"Find your own way of attending, and not worry about listening to my voice. As I'm talking, you don't need to worry about my words, my meanings, my intentions, because you can enjoy learning how to attend to the things that are important. As I've been speaking, your body has settled, but you don't need to worry about that; your breathing has changes, and your blinking has changed, but you don't need to worry about that. There are so many things that you don't need to worry about, that you can really enjoy the experience of simply being here, as you are, feeling more and more how you might want to feel."*

Should someone be kept awake by *physical discomfort or pain* then it is expected that what's missing might be *physical comfort, not noticing the sensations, or attending more fully to them so they blend with the background experience.* A hypnotic session might include *"As you sit in that chair, you can enjoy the comfort of knowing that for this time there is nothing special you need to do. You don't need to notice the comfort of your feet on the floor, you don't need to notice the increasing comfort that can begin to spread through your body, and it could be a relief when you don't even notice the way my voice and various other sensations can blend with the background of your experience so you don't need to notice that, and instead, enjoy the increasing comfort of letting yourself learn from this experience anything that will be useful for you and your future well being."*

Some clients complain that even though they *feel tired,* they *don't feel sleepy.* I have found it helpful to make the distinction between tiredness and sleepiness, reminding such clients that we have all felt sleepy when bored – a bad lecture or a slow moving film, when we weren't tired, so it shouldn't be surprising that we can on occasions feel tired without feeling sleepy. This shifts the focus, and we can then see that *sleepiness* is what's missing, not relaxation, comfort, or peace of mind. We can invite such a client to *"Close your eyes and begin to discover how boring my voice can become, and that the more you try to listen to every word, the more and more bored and sleepy you become. And as that sleepiness increases, you can learn that experience and use it at some future time, whenever it is useful to you."* Strategies can also be helpful here. I have helped all of my children to sleep when they couldn't by the simple suggestion that they close their eyes and try to stay awake for as long as possible. Mostly they don't succeed for long.

Difficulties Staying Asleep
When a client is troubled by *waking after going to sleep*, it can be helpful to invite this person into hypnosis, then have them come out of hypnosis so they can discover how easy it can be *"To let yourself drift back into hypnosis, by remembering the natural ease you felt a moment ago, and as you recall that experience, it can be a pleasure to go into hypnosis, perhaps even deeper than before."* The we can repeat the process again with the suggestion that *"Every time you wake out of hypnosis, it can be even easier to go even deeper into hypnosis."* By providing an experience such as this, we can offer a metaphoric communication, which could be made explicit, that the same applies to going back to sleep.

When a dog began to bark every night about 2.00 am, waking me up, I grew tired of being disturbed, and began to think that the dog was trying to be helpful to me by singing me a lullaby. This, along with many other similar experiences informs my approach when someone seeks help with *external noises wake them*. In the hypnotic session, we can suggest to such a client that *"You can let your own internal comfort continually increase, and enjoy discovering that the sound of my voice, along with other external noises here, can blend with the background so that they can actually allow you to feel more comfortable and at ease than silence."* It might be helpful to add in metaphors about the way that people who live near airports don't hear the planes, those who live on a busy road soon learn how to block out traffic noise. One of my favourite examples is about a woman whose husband's snoring was waking her up. She became so infuriated with the fact that he was a sleep while she was awake and she said to herself that the louder he snored, the deeper she could sleep. And she did, and continues to do so.

When my son was much younger, he woke one night knowing that if he tried to get back to sleep the same monster that had been trying to harm him would be there waiting for him. I told him that monsters were furious with children because they never asked the monster what its name was. The next morning my son was rather bored to report to me that, yes, the monster had returned, and yes, he had asked its name, and yes, he had even asked the monster if it would like a cup of tea. My son was bored, and the monster hasn't returned.

Conclusion

Treating individuals as individuals, exploring the individuality of their problems; helping them to create individual solutions; these attitudes prevent us becoming trapped in a mechanistic one-size-fits-all approach, adds to the effectiveness of the results, and contributes to the satisfaction of the therapist.

Rob McNeilly

Erickson's contribution, at first viewed as radical, is now mainstream, and continues to invite interested practitioners to enjoy the privilege of the therapeutic process.

In particular, inquiring into what's missing for any individual who presents with sleeping difficulties will add to the effectiveness of our interventions to get out of their own way and enjoy again the benefit of natural, spontaneous experience of sleeping.

References

(1) Brochure

(2) Personal communication 1977

(3) McNeilly RB, Healing the Whole Person: A Solution-Focused Approach to Using Positive Language, Emotions, and Actions in Therapy, New York: John Wiley & Sons, Inc. Publishers, June 2000.

A Place To Learn In - A Place To Teach From

Introduction

Finding ways of connecting with our students and putting our own limitations aside will be a major concern to any serious teacher. Although we all appreciate the importance of these opportunities, and achieve them sometimes, we are left with the dilemma of how we can create them more predictably. "The Clearing" and "The Space of Nothingness" are two places to visit so we can explore these possibilities.

The Clearing

Heidegger spoke of "lichtung" or lightening which also brings a mood of lightness and is translated as "the clearing." This refers to the experience of walking in a forest, and suddenly "seeing" the forest as the forest. The forest appears out of the background, where we were unaware of it. We may have been thinking about something, feeling hungry, tired, excited, but unaware of the forest with our attention elsewhere. When we "see" the forest, we connect with it in a novel and holistic way. We are in a clearing – not a clearing like an absence of trees, but rather seeing that all the trees are there as part of the forest and seeing the forest as a totality – and there is something sacred about this experience, the sacredness of connecting with something greater or beyond ourselves. We could also call this a spiritual experience.

In "The Clearing" we disappear as an observer, and there is nothing between us and the forest. It is as if we, as observers, are not there. We are so present that we become part of the forest, and it doesn't make sense to speak of us or the forest – we and the forest become "We-in-the-forest" to follow Heidegger. We become transparent.

Each clearing brings with it a unique set of assumptions, emotions, distinctions and observations, as well as its blindness, and there are as many clearings as there are observers. A group of people could enter a room, and the one room would show up very differently. An electrician might notice the lights, switches, power points. A decorator might notice the colour scheme, the style of the furniture, the ambience. A musician might notice the room's acoustic properties, while a building inspector might be more interested in R.S.J.'s and position of fire extinguishers. Each would bring a coherent set of observations and look within that set, often unaware that they are observing from within that set, or there are other sets of observations or distinctions. They would usually be unaware of the particular observer that they happen to be, i.e. the particular clearing that that individual is standing in. In any clearing, the assumptions are given, obvious, unquestioned and so, transparent.

We are always in some sort of clearing, attending to some cluster of concerns, taking care of some collection of issues. Recognising this allows us to observe the clearing we happen to be in, and influence this by settling into it if it is a helpful clearing, or shifting to another, preferred clearing, by designing the shifting process and becoming more familiar with the desired clearing as well as the shifting process itself.

Because clearings are sets of distinctions in which we will be oriented towards taking care of certain concerns, predisposed to take certain clusters of actions, all of which will be related, consistent and coherent, clearings are related to emotions. "The Clearing" can usefully be placed in the domain of language since it is concerned with coordination of future action (Maturana's definition of language) and just as usefully placed in the emotional domain since it evokes corresponding predispositions for action (Maturana's definition of emotions). To add to the texture, we could also place it in the body domain, since different clearings will call forth different bodihoods from the individual. More important than placing it in one or other classification is to appreciate the richness of the notion.

A Learning Clearing

Learning can be a clearing in itself. In a learning clearing, that is to say when learning is happening as a transparent phenomenon, a whole variety of assumptions is operating in the background, usually unquestioned. To learn, we are already assuming that we don't know something, and are willing to learn. We give authority to the teacher, putting our trust in the teacher. We put aside any prejudices we may have about the subject, our abilities, what we already know. We give ourselves permission to be a beginner; to make mistakes, to be corrected, to make the same mistakes as many times as it takes for us to adapt and learn. This provides for the opportunity for a new observer to emerge as a result of the learning, as an expression of that learning.

How Can We Design A Clearing?

Just as we can put ourselves in a situation where we are more likely to feel this way or that, we can put ourselves in our habitual teaching clearing and allow the ongoing interactions to happen spontaneously.

Such an experience might begin by allowing ourselves to become more attentive to external experiences – sights, sounds, smells – and at the same time less aware of internal experiences – we don't need to notice our feet on the floor, our increasing comfort, the easy rhythm of our breathing.

We could then recall the way we first began to learn to walk, or write, or ride a bicycle when we were able to give less and less attention to the mechanics of the process, and begin to allow the walking, etc., to become a more automatic function as we attended more fully to where we were walking, what we were writing, the journey as we rode the bicycle. This allowing of the awareness of the actions to drift into the background is mirrored in Erickson's comments about a learning "Dropping into your unconscious." We let go of the attention on the self and are freed to respond more fully to our surroundings – the ground, chairs, doors, bumps in the road, nuances of meaning ...

I have noticed that when I first began to teach, that it was easy to lose track of the student. I was so intent on getting it right, sticking to the theory, that I could even forget that the student was there, although such students were well aware of my absence. As the learning settled in, or as I settled into the learning, the way of speaking just happens and I don't need to plan my sentences, the session – it begins to flow. It begins to flow just as our walking or writing flow.

A professional violinist was contemplating giving up his career because of increasing tension in his shoulders. He was comforted to be reminded that he had been playing that music for long enough to learn it thoroughly, so the next time he played publicly, he could tuck the violin under his chin and *let the violin play the music*. He could enjoy listening to the result, without any effort. A professional golfer overcame his putting problem by imagining that there was a groove in the green and the ball could easily roll along that groove into the hole. Perhaps he wouldn't even need to hit the ball, the ball might somehow get the club to hit it. Several years later, he was able to extend this learning and hit two holes in one at one tournament.

When I was a discussant at the first International Ericksonian Congress, the third speaker began his presentation by announcing that although he had prepared a paper, he was not going to talk about it. This threw me into a panic since my prepared comments suddenly became irrelevant. When he sat down, and I stood facing a sea of 2000 faces of world experts and had nothing to say, I could only open my mouth and listen to the words that emerged. Several people complimented me afterwards about the helpfulness of my comments. As Red

Smith, an American sports writer said, "Writing's easy. I just sit at the typewriter and open a vein."

We are, after all, all connected – all part of this universe. We all contain the common elements from the big bang all those eons ago, so it make perfect sense to see the connection between the fluttering of a butterfly's wings in the Amazon valley and a storm off the coast of Northern Scotland.

We can then wonder about how we can let go into this wonder, allow ourselves to trust ourselves to make the mistakes we can learn from, and explore the infinite possibilities our experience offers us in the process of teaching.

The Space Of Nothingness

Visiting "The Clearing" is one way of connecting with the student. In visiting "The Space of Nothingness" we can explore a place for us to let go of any personal attitudes, which might limit the student's potential for learning.

Creating requires that we begin with nothing - anything else is mere rearrangement. We can only create a new house if we first clear the block or we are renovating. We can only create a new document if we begin with a blank page, otherwise we are editing.

One of the key characteristics of any form of effective teaching and learning is creativity – to get past any preconceptions of how a student *should* be, change, respond, learn, and be open to them as they are. One option is to begin with some formulation, diagnostic schema, or pre-planned teaching format and apply it – a rearrangement of the student (always for their benefit, but from the wisdom and power of the teacher). Erickson invited us into another approach - to give the student as much opportunity as possible to explore their own experience, their own resources, their own learning goals and methods. This process is creative and requires that we remove anything in the way, so there is then *nothing* in our way of assisting the student to achieve their experience of having *nothing* preventing them from learning what they need, becoming how they wish, or perhaps really are.

Lao Tzu wrote 2 ½ thousand years ago in Chapter 11 of his Tao Te Ching:

> "Thirty spokes share the wheel's hub;
> It is the centre hole that makes it useful.
> Shape clay into a vessel;
> It is the space within that makes it useful.
> Cut doors and windows for a room;
> It is the holes which make it useful.
> Therefore profit comes from what is there;
> Usefulness from what is not there."

We recurrently acknowledge the prime importance of listening and yet, knowing this, we still get distracted by our own thoughts, plans, knowing … knowing that these relate to us and not the student is insufficient to stop them. Finding some way to let go of our prejudices, our hopes, our wishes, will allow room for the student's to emerge and take shape. One way of taking care of this continuing concern will be to visit "The Space of Nothingness," where we can let go of anything that is in the student's way will be an area of learning.

We can appreciate this, so why is it so difficult, or even near to impossible at times? A colleague reported feeling uncomfortable, saying she felt I was "teaching *at* her" in a conversation. Her comments had the effect of quieting my thoughts about what *should* be happening, and the resulting space, or *nothing*, opened my seeing of her so she actually appeared out of the blurred perception of her that I had unwittingly created. In getting to *nothing* I could put aside my projections, so we could begin to create a useful and relevant learning interaction together.

How often do our students tolerate us not listening, hoping that one day, someone, anyone, *ANYONE* might see them, hear them, teach them?

This brings the question "How can we listen to a student, when we are attuned to listening to our own thoughts about the student?" and invites exploration of quieting, if not silencing our thoughts, or perhaps loosening our attachment to them. How can we get to visit this "Space of Nothingness?"

When I read Lao Tzu, chapter 56 of Tao Te Ching: "Those that know do not talk. Those that talk do not know" I was perplexed. Did that mean that any time I said something I was placing myself in the company of those who didn't know? It seemed to be a bind. The relief came when I remembered Erickson's invitation to "observe, observe, observe." This willingness to listen without the need to say anything, can allow us to say what is there to say, without trying to force the issue from a position of the expert. Listening allows for the sensitive response to the environment, the student's environment, so that our response related to the student, is relevant to the student, is a function of the student, not of our own expertise. How can we actually achieve this? How can we ensure that our thinking and speaking doesn't interfere with our listening to our student? Perhaps sometimes silence?

Various writers have commented about this issue. The entry for January 14th 2001 in The Dalai Lama's Book of Daily meditations is: "Sometimes one creates a dynamic impression by saying something. And sometimes one creates as significant an impression by remaining silent." Wittgenstein's words "Whereof one cannot speak, thereof one should pass in silence," while they invite silence, also hint, to me, at a respectful listening without trying to explain, and in a mood of wonder and acceptance. Lao Tzu again points to this in chapter 64 of Tao Te Ching: "Knowing nothing needs to be done is the place we begin to move from" and this doesn't necessarily mean we should sit paralysed, but rather to avoid pushing the river, and merely be part of the river's natural tendency to remove any obstacles in its path so there is then *nothing* in the way of the natural flow. From Lao Tzu again in chapter 32, "Tao in the world is like a river flowing home to the sea."

In "The Clearing" we can find ways to connect, blend, meld, merge with the other (person, forest, experience), allowing us to have the experience of *nothing* separating us - no boundaries, and permits an immediate gateway into a sacred realm. For me, this is the place to listen from, a place where listing becomes possible.

But there's always *something*. This has even become a cliché. If it's not the gas bill, it's the car registration. If it's not the cleaning, it's the painting. If it's not the lawn, it's the garden - always *something* in the way of the *nothing* that we seek.

Also we humans are so intriguingly ambivalent. We can hang out for a holiday, and when it happens, we get bored. We are desperate for THE relationship, only to find ourselves singing the line from Peggy Lee - "Is that all there is? ..."

We know the bliss of *nothing* but seem to fall into filling that *nothing* with *something*, even *anything*. Just as nature abhors a vacuum, human nature abhors the experience of *nothing*. So there is an area for learning, for exploration, for wondering that emerges from this dilemma - how can we get past the *something*, the *anything*, and experience *nothing* so that what we are seeking has at least the possibility of appearing?

A person can sit, and even though there can be sensations, there isn't really any need to attend to those sensations that don't require attention. They can be there, somewhere in the background, but they can be ignored. Even though they are there, it can be as if they aren't there at all.

A person can be reading, attending to the experience, having their own thought, making their own connections, creating their own learning, and at the same time, there is no need to count the words, recognise individual letters. They can disappear into the general experience of attending to the images, and even though there are many potential diversions, these diversions seem to disappear and the texture, the experience of the story itself can be where the attention simply finds itself.

The same person can listen to music, to the sounds of nature, to the silence of a sunset, and even though there may be other sounds, even though there may be the sounds that are there, or the silence, all this can become background, and only the important and relevant sounds or lack of sounds can be what is attended to.

It is also possible for sensations, stories, pleasurable sounds to also begin to disappear, so then a rather delightful numbness, a sense of peace, and a silence can be there, perhaps the kind of peaceful silence that we could experience if we were in the middle of outer space, or in the middle of inner space, or in the middle of nowhere, or in the middle of somewhere, without needing or even wanting to be concerned about inner or outer, somewhere or nowhere, but simply, peacefully, completely freed and immersed in the experience with nothing happening to disturb the fullness of the sense of peace and completeness.

We can look at the night sky, imagine being somewhere there, nowhere in particular, and watch the universe turn slowly and silently around that experience, and in the experience of allowing such an experience, we can only wonder what might appear in the spaces between the planets; in the spaces between the stars, in the spaces between the spaces as we could look out into the infinite space that the universe is. To be in this experience and then return from it can be an opportunity to look with fresh eyes, listen with fresh ears, experience some event, place, person or interaction and experience it as if for the first time, with nothing in the way of that freshness, that newness, that immediacy.

As you experience whatever is happening at any moment, there is no need to attend to the experience in any particular way; no need to attend to sensations that are of no concern; no need to attend to noises that are not relevant; but simply, relaxedly, effortlessly, allow the experience that is happening to be an experience that can in some way become a space for some new appreciating, some new recognition, some new opportunities to appear, as if from nowhere, not needing to have a use that is immediately apparent, and perhaps only after, or not even then, so that in some way, there can be more room, more space more opportunities to experience the wonder, the miraculous possibilities, the subtle and delightful experiences that are there, that we are, waiting to be experienced, whenever we take the time, create the space, allow the opportunity for whatever that might be to become visible, to appear out of nowhere, or somewhere, or wherever, so we have an opportunity to see them, to hear them, to experience them.

We can find ourselves sitting with a student, becoming absorbed in their experience, and allow any of our own thoughts, our own ideas, our own images, to drift into some silence, so not only can we disappear as an entity, not only can the student disappear as an entity, not only the floor, the walls, the ceiling, the furniture disappear into that same space, but there can then be an experience of total spaciousness and peace, which can then be experienced in any way that is of benefit, or value or use to the student, as they connect in their own way with their own resourcefulness – with the resourcefulness of the universe which surrounds them, and us, and contains an infinite variety of opportunities for learning, for developing, for experiencing.

And as with so many experiences, it's never necessary to fully or even partially recognise or understand the process of experiencing precisely what is needed to have that become a part of our reality, because, after all, reality belongs to the universe, and it can be such a wondrous delight to explore some small aspect of what that might be, and how it might relate to us and to our future – individually and shared.

It is possible, then to have some awareness of this experience and have it exactly where it needs to be to be accessible, always with a sense of peace and fulfillment. And that is why I want to thank you for the opportunity to share this experience with you, and the less of me, the more of you can be available for your experience of what can be useful and relevant and satisfying for you, your future and your teaching and learning.

Conclusion

"The Clearing" is the direction of connecting with the student, and "The Space of Nothingness" is the place we begin to connect from.

Stopping Smoking:
Does It Have To Be Difficult?

Smoking is increasingly out of fashion in Australia, as in US, although Europe is still to make the move. I recall walking through a smoking carriage in Denmark several years ago and could hardly see the far end – a passive smoker's nightmare. It's hard to imagine that a mere 100 years ago the medical profession which is so evangelically against cigarettes were prescribing the evil weed for neurasthenia!

Many people stop smoking simply by stopping, and not much is heard about this, and of course, many more never start. It seems that teenagers are still drawn to the experience, presumably for the sorts of reasons that teenagers are drawn to anything – belonging, rebelling, dealing with the ambiguities and hypocrisies of the "adult" world which doers its best to seduce them with advertising then criticises them if the advertising is successful.

Hypnosis is one way for those who have started, for whatever reason, and want to stop, for whatever reason, and experience difficulty to find a solution.

Hypnosis is at last becoming accepted as a legitimate approach to resolving human dilemmas. Traditionally it has been associated with mind control, reprogramming, and entertainment, with all the expected concerns for the recipient of being taken over, changed, damaged. The traditional approach grew out of an era 100 years ago where domination, patriarchal control, and force were everywhere. In our contemporary society, collaboration and customer satisfaction take precedence and so the solution orientation to hypnosis appeared.

This orientation to hypnosis, pioneered by the American psychiatrist, Milton Erickson, emphasises a person's resource-fullness, and rather than trying to force a change of thinking by repeatedly imposing incantations to do this, not that, seeks to evoke from within the person themselves a connection with their own innate capacities. This approach has a very different mood – one of respectful and collaborative expectancy – and can add tremendously to the mutual satisfaction of all involved as well as to the effectiveness.

When I first learnt about hypnosis, I learnt that you "put someone" into hypnosis, gave them suggestions, and then "took them out" of hypnosis, something like a general anesthetic. After Erickson, I recognised that people are so different, and it became imperative to find out who this person is, how come they want to stop smoking, why now, what have cigarettes been doing for them, what have they already tried that didn't work, where did they get the idea that hypnosis could help. I have found that these questions help to connect each individual person with their own individual experiences and have massively enhanced the effectiveness of the process. Instead of a one-size-fits-all approach, the hypnotic experience can be tailored to each the individual, ensuring a good fit.

Hypnosis has traditionally been a set procedure administered by an expert. After Erickson, however, the process is more like a conversation that invites each person to focus and become absorbed in their own individual way so that the changes facilitated by their hypnotic experiences can match their desires, hopes and satisfy their individual concerns.

A man in his 40s wanted to stop smoking for health reasons, was thinking obsessively about cigarettes and what they were doing to him, and feeling guilty that he was still smoking. He also complained that his bad memory was interfering with his business – he couldn't remember the names of regular customers. In the hypnotic session, he was complimented about his ability to forget names, and responded to the idea that he could forget about smoking. He let the thought of smoking go from his awareness and by the time he had stopped smoking completely, about 2 weeks, his memory had improved considerably and he was relieved on both fronts.

A woman told me that she had begun to smoke as a teenager due to peer pressure, and now all her friends were stopping smoking. Being a non-smoker was the thing to do now. She somewhat reluctantly admitted that her breathing was mildly effected due to the cigarettes. By assisting her to focus on her breathing, and the pleasure of breathing, she was able to become more absorbed in that experience and began to give less attention to outside noises and the random thoughts which we all normally have. She became increasingly comfortable as the time continued, and she enjoyed the experience as if she had already become a non-smoker, including the enjoyment of breathing easily, but particularly the relief of pressure from her friends now that she was fitting in, once again.

A man enjoyed being a wine connoisseur and although he was determined to stop smoking, he was concerned that his enjoyment of wine may diminish, since it had become a habit to smoke with wine during and after a pleasant meal. He was worried that he might have to stop drinking, which he loved, and that when he had wine, his will power might decrease, and he'd begin smoking again. He readily became absorbed in the pleasure of imagining that he was sipping his favourite wine, closed his eyes to add to the degree of absorption, and was encouraged to enjoy the flavour even more now that his palate was clear of cigarette smoke. He was encouraged to imagine himself at some specific future meal, enjoying his wine as a non-smoker, and he was amused to notice that when he became aware that someone at a nearby table was smoking (in this imagined restaurant), that he became irritated that this interfered with his sipping pleasure. He was relieved by this recognition, and left confident.

A woman said she was concerned about her appearance, specially the fine lines on her face that she attributed to decades of smoking. She spoke of wrinkled skin like a smoked sardine. She was keen to stop smoking, but spoke of some reluctance because she had heard that some people gain weight after stopping, and this was something she emphatically wanted to avoid. She was invited to recall her recent holiday where she was away from the pressures of her high flying managerial position, and as she focused on this and became absorbed, she was able to imagine that time had passed, she was now a non-smoker, her skin was smooth, her weight was fine, and she reported that she felt an intense feeling of relief, which is a common result of hypnosis. I offered the idea that as a non-smoker, her taste buds would be more sensitive, and so she would have greater taste satisfaction with less food, and expressed my concern that she may even lose some weight, hoping it wouldn't be enough to have her skin become wrinkled with the loss. She was very pleased.

At no time were these people told anything, or warned of the dangers or down side of smoking. They were each respected as individuals doing what they could, and looking for some resource that would allow them to achieve what they wished. There were no scripts, but each person was honoured as a unique individual, and their wishes were legitimised, and their personal styles used as a basis for the change they wished. This is such a contrast to the stereotyped but still occurring picture of a charismatic hypnotist, usually male, emphatically ordering some behaviour, or commanding in an authoritarian manner that some passive person will respond to some sort of psychological surgery where the cigarette smoking is excised.

Years ago I saw an episode of "Minder" on TV where Arthur Daly had hypnosis to stop smoking cigars. He was instructed that they would taste like burnt rubber, expecting that this would put him off. Not our Arthur. By the end of the episode he was saying that he thought he could get used to the taste of burnt rubber.

After Erickson, such coarse manipulation became unnecessary, even distasteful, and we can now assist people, with a more respectful hypnotic experience, to access their own individual resources, and achieve a result that suits them, in a manner and time that is theirs. It's a pleasure to be part of that process.

Creating A Context For Therapy: Is There Anything Else?

Abstract:

What is the purpose of therapy? What is therapy? Is it about finding some techniques of one or other school of psychotherapy or some other source to change some circumstances, whether internal or external to the client, related to some problem? Is it possible to distil from the disparate epistemologies some core structure to guide the therapist? Or is it something else? This paper addresses that something else - a possible underlying principle or state, to which may be added - a context. Could this context then be something shared by the client and therapist within which the process of allowing the interaction of the content of the situation to occur and from which a new perspective could evolve? Is this context some chance experience i.e. a content or could it be created? The purpose of this paper is to question some of this.

I would like to begin this paper by quoting Wittgenstein[1] "My propositions are elucidatory in this way: he who understands me finally recognises them as senseless, when he has climbed out through them, on them, over them. (He must so to speak throw away the ladder after he has climbed up on it). He must surmount these propositions; then he sees the world rightly. Whereof one cannot speak, thereof one must be silent."

What then is the purpose of therapy? Surely it is about change - but of what? Certainly it must have to do with a problem - but what is a problem? A flat tyre may appear as a problem to a motorist but to a tyre repairer it is just the opposite. Is it some circumstance outside the client (i.e. a content); is it some difficulty in coping with or avoiding stress (i.e. a process)? Is the purpose to have the therapist do something to or for the client? This may be especially relevant in those specifically seeking hypnotherapy, with its myths of control, and is there any hope of avoiding the ego trip of the hypnotherapist? Robert Shaw[2] of the Centre for Contextual Therapy is described as "non attached" in the sense that the therapist's ego is not dependent on the outcome of any case. The cautionary comment that people seek therapy not to overcome problems but to refine them is apposite to each. Erickson[3] had this to say in the foreword to "Change" - "Psychotherapy is sought not primarily for enlightenment about the unchangeable past but because of dissatisfaction with the present and a desire to better the future." How often during therapy does the purpose of the therapy alter so that the originally stated purpose becomes irrelevant? Perhaps this is best attended by keeping the question open throughout therapy.

What is therapy? This will be related to the perceived purpose of the therapy and its interaction with concepts and theories which evolve from the perceptions of the various schools of therapy, and these schools can show amazingly disparate epistemologies. At the Evolution of Psychotherapy Conference in Phoenix in 1985 attended by 7,000 health professionals, 15 major schools of therapy were counted excluding Szasz and including Wolpe, Rogers, Ellis, Bettelheim, R.D. Laing, Rollo May, Jay Haley and Virginia Satir. Zeig who organised and participated in the congress thought it had helped to produce some "baby steps" towards consensus. There are, in addition, many other therapies, including physical therapies, naturopathy, chiropractic, which have their psychological effect. Each school has its own complex explanation for pathology and hence its own jargon and rationalisation of treatment approaches which are self-reinforcing in a circular way.

It seems, then, little short of miraculous that in spite of this ever increasing variety, successes and failures do occur in each of these schools and leads one to wonder how (perhaps even if) the results are related to the particular approach or is it something else. The founders of these schools have been investigated by interested, sometimes fanatically devoted, followers who, though they may elucidate some aspect of the founder, fail to reproduce either him or his results and the very variability of these is testimony to that.

Few people would deny the enormous contribution to psychotherapy and hypnotherapy that Milton Erickson provided and yet in spite of the still increasing writing about his work he remains an original and not able to be copied. Haley[4,5] has written of his strategic approach, Bandler and Grinder[6,7] of his language structure in relation to transderivational grammar, Rossi[8,9,10] of intrapsychic processes, Rosen[11] and Gordon[12] of his use of stories and metaphors but Erickson remains the best source of Ericksonian therapy and Zeig[13,14] also Rossi[15,16] provide opportunities to experience him directly without any superimposed structure.

Since it seems apparent that there is something else other than the content, process and interpretations (theories) of therapy, it may be of acute relevance to ask what is this something else? When some therapeutic interchange is occurring, clearly there is no theory operating, but rather the interchange is occurring and perhaps afterwards it may be interpreted. Even if some clinical plan is formed before the exchange, what happens happens, which may or may not then be seen to be related to the plan?

Could this be called the context of therapy? - The space within which, the background against which the therapy occurs if it does.

The Oxford Dictionary[17] defines context as "the parts which immediately precede or follow any particular passage or text and determine its meaning" while Bateson[18,19] distinguishes between epistemology or the study of how we know what we know and ontology or the study of how things are e.g. the menu is clearly distinct from the meal and it would be tragic if that distinction were not made. Perhaps some of the difficulties we experience in discussion, in therapy, and in life stem from not making this distinction and perhaps it may be most relevant to make it. An essential element of any meal is the unknown about it. If it were totally predictable then the pleasure would be lessened and even if the meal is as was expected, perhaps there is relief in discovering that the uncertainty about its quality, having set up the experience, then allows for its appearance by the disappearance of the uncertainty.

What is the context of this conference? Is it the location or the programme, or the organisers or the participants whether speaking or listening? Perhaps it is none of these but something else. Perhaps a willingness to discover something already known at some level but unknown in the usual way. Perhaps a willingness to not know.

Lao Tzu[20] says:

56.   "Those who know do not talk.
       Those who talk do not know."

I would have to hope that there is some other way of hearing that other than the way it may be heard.

And again

48.   "In the pursuit of learning, every day
       something is acquired.
       In the pursuit of Tao, every day
       something is dropped.
       Less and less is done.
       Until non-action is achieved.
       When nothing is done, nothing is left undone.
       The world is ruled by letting things
       take their course.
       It cannot be ruled by interfering."

15.   "The ancient masters were subtle,

mysterious, profound, responsive.

The depth of their knowledge is unfathomable.

Because it is unfathomable,

All we can do is describe their appearance."

In particular:

11.   "Thirty spokes share the wheel's hub;

It is the centre hole that makes it useful.

Shape clay into a vessel;

It is the space within that makes it useful.

Cut doors and windows for a room;

It is the holes which make it useful.

Therefore profit comes from what is there;

Usefulness from what is not there."

Maturana[21] a biologist whose work may, after Erickson, have the next major impact on therapy, both individual and family, removes the mystery with his theory of "Structural Determinism." He states that a living system's operation is determined by its structure, is informationally closed, has a career which consists entirely of a purposeless drift and occurs in a reality which he describes as "objectivity in parenthesis" - an "as if" reality.

Shakespeare's Macbeth says of life ......

"It is a tale told by an idiot,

full of sound and furry,

Signifying nothing."

This somewhat depressing attitude is transformed into a vast range of possibilities when one recognises that to ascribe meaning (depression) to meaninglessness is not only meaningless but absurd.

It follows then that a therapist claiming to change a client is arrogant and even absurd and that the best that can be attempted is to drift with the client in such a way that in the drifting some internal perturbations can occur within the client which can then sometimes lead to change. Dell[22] points out that a resistant or obnoxious patient is "simply being who he or she is. What we find obnoxious is the fact that the patient is not as we want him or her to be."

(Frankl)[23] describes a case of a depressed widower who was stuck in a grief reaction to his wife's death. It was pointed out to him that her death saved her from the anguish of coping with his death and that shift in the context totally transformed his experience. In "Change" Watzlawick, Weakland and Fisch[24] discuss the problem of frigidity in an aggressive female being redefined as an attempt to protect her husband from her uninhibited sexuality, is asked "what if he becomes impotent?" And is thanked for her efforts to help him.

Can this context, which allows change to occur within the individual, be created or is it just some chance happening? Schrodinger[25] states "Every man's world picture is and always remains a constrict of his mind and cannot be proved to have any other existence," and raises the question - not "can it be created?" But rather can any experience ever be other than created? Perhaps this created context can be found not in finding answers but in a continuing willingness to not know, to question one's underlying associations - beliefs, prejudices, opinions, theories, attachments, etc. - and live in the uncertainty that is. This is made more challenging since they may be profoundly not visible to us - it is impossible to see one's seeing, to listen to one's listening - and perhaps the closest we can get is to be willing to say no to anything known as a "truth." In this immediate situation it may be relevant to question whether I am being heard or is each individual here creating, perhaps inventing, their own version of me and what I am saying. Erickson[26] advises "... in psychotherapy you listen to your patient, knowing that you don't understand the personal meanings of his vocabulary .... so you listen to your patient knowing his personal meaning. And he doesn't know your personal meaning for words. You try to understand the patient's words as he understands them." Egendorf,[27] in the preface to "Healing from the War. Trauma and Transformation after Vietnam" does not see "healing as a process" but "I see it occur in special moments discontinuously, not in a smooth flow. Apprehending this point enables people to recognise that any and every moment can be a profound opportunity in their lives."

Is there anything else apart from context? Yes - the techniques, processes, theories, manipulations, strategies, drug therapies, physical therapies, family interactions. These may now be able to be seen as content within a context of what may be possible.

"From break of day
Till sunset glow
I toil.
I dig my well,
I plow my field,
And earn my food
And drink.
What care I
Who rules the world
If I am left in peace."
Poet unknown[28] Ca 2300 B.C.

Lao Tzu writes:

32.   "Once the whole is divided, the
        parts need names.
        There are already enough names.
        One must know when to stop.
        Knowing when to stop averts trouble.
        Tao in the world is like a river flowing
        home to the sea."

So that it why I would like to begin by quoting Wittgenstein[1] "My propositions are elucidatory in this way: he who understands me finally recognises them as senseless, when he has climbed out through them, on them, over them. (He must so to speak throw away the ladder after he has climbed up on it). He must surmount these propositions; then he sees the world rightly. Whereof one cannot speak, thereof one must be silent."

References

(1) Wittgenstein, Tractus Logico-Philosophicils

(2) Shaw, The Family Networker May-June 1986 P.54

(3) Watzlawick Weakland & Fisch, Change Principles of Problem Formation and Problem Resolution

(4) Haley, Uncommon Therapy

(5) Haley, Conversations with Milton H. Erickson Vol. I, II & III

(6) Bandler and Grinder, The Structure of Magic Vol. I & II

(7) The Patterns of the Hypnotic Techniques of Milton H. Erickson M.D. Vol. I & II

(8) Rossi, Hypnotic Realities

(9) Rossi, Hypnotherapy, An Exploratory Casebook

(10) Rossi, Experiencing Hypnosis

(11) Rosen, My Voice Will Go With You

(12) Gordon, Metaphors

(13) Zeig, A Teaching Seminar with Milton H. Erickson

(14) Zeig, Experiencing Erickson

(15) Rossi, Healing in Hypnosis

(16) Rossi, Life Reframing

(17) Shorter Oxford Dictionary

(18) Bateson, Steps to an Ecology of Mind P.313

(19) Bateson, Steps to an Ecology of Mind P.154

(20) Lao Tzu, Tao Te Ching

(21) Maturana, The Family Networker May-June 1985 P.24

(22) Dell, Family Process, P.30

(23) Frankl, Man's Search for Meaning

(24) Watzlawick Weakland & Fisch, Change - Principles of Problem Formation and Problem Resolution, P.102

(25) Schrodinger, Mind and Matter

(26) Zeig (Ed) A Teaching Seminar with Milton H. Erickson P.158

(27) Egendorf, Healing from the War - Trauma and Transformation after Vietnam, Preface

(28) Weiner-David, Of Things Most Yielding 53P.60

The Emerging Language Of Emotions
And The Body

Therapists and other human beings know about emotions and their importance. We all know that we have a body. But what are emotions? What is the relevance of the body? How can we integrate them into therapy?

These are questions we have been concerned with since the beginning of therapy conversations, and there are many differing understandings in the field.

Emotions – Another View
Traditionally emotions have been regarded either as they are bodily fluids which build up, need releasing, needing to be expressed rather than repressed, or alternatively, as sign posts of issues lurking beneath the surface requiring exploration. While these approaches continue to be valuable, even curative at times, there is an additional view which can contribute to our clinical effectiveness.

This additional view emerges from the thinking of Maturana, and some of his past Chilean students – Echeverria, Flores, and Olalla. They propose that emotions can usefully be explored as predispositions to actions, or domains of actions, and like Heidegger used "languaging" to express the action aspect of language, they offer "emotioning" to remind us of this dynamic. The word "emotion" has "motion" as its core, implying action, and our common sense observation informs us that we are variably predisposed to act in various emotions.

When we are in an emotion of confidence, there are a vastly different cluster of actions available to us from that of fear. When we are peaceful, we act very differently from when we are frustrated. Even the expression "We are peaceful" points to the central influence of emotions – in an emotion of peace, we *are* a certain way.

More Options For The Therapist

Observing emotions this way gives us an additional set of observations, and as a direct result, an additional set of possible interventions in working with clients. The more observations we are able to make, the more options for intervening will appear to us, the more use we will be to clients.

Brief, Solution Oriented therapy has been criticised for being cerebral, mechanistic, and emotionless, prompting Cade & O'Hanlon (1993) to dedicate a chapter to emotions, but these authors limit their comments to the essential need to acknowledge and validate clients' emotions. While this brings emotions into the field, they don't take the next step of exploring the associated actions and the possible shifting of the experience at an emotional level.

I have found (McNeilly 2000) a predictable value in exploring some finer details of emotions which have been clustered in unhelpful groups. In the arena of anger, for example, I like to explore the differences between resentment, frustration, indignation, and rage. By observing the actions we are predisposed to in resentment, for example, a silent promise for revenge following some past damage of importance is often reported. Of course, different individuals will have their individual experience, but many report something similar. These observations open conversations about the validity of the past damage, a questioning of its present importance, an exploration of the value of sacrificing the self for the sake of getting revenge on another, and so, a wider range of options. The possibility of forgiveness may appear, perhaps for a selfish reason rather than as a "should" for a good person, since it can relieve the suffering of the resenter.

Frustration is usually accompanied or constituted of some stifled expressiveness, and exemplifies the value of emotional release as a predictably useful action.

Indignation is a very different emotion, while still in the realm of anger. It is commonly expressed as a cluster of actions which protect the space or dignity of the client in the presence of some potential damage similar to some which have been troublesome in the past. In my view, indignation is to be enhanced as a solution, never a problem.

Rage, which is feared by any sane human being, is frequently experienced as an indiscriminate predisposition to damage anything and everyone without concern for consequences, which is why we fear it and if resentment and frustration are effectively dealt with, and indignation enhanced, then rage could be lessened or prevented.

More Options For The Client

Conversations following the question "When you are anxious/depressed/terrified/uncertain, what are you doing in that situation?" can be usefully insightful to clients, allowing them to see some things which were previously not apparent to them. It's not uncommon for a client to recognise their actions for the first time, and this can be sufficient to break the pattern of doing.

New Options For The Therapy

As well as exploring the doing aspect of some limiting emotion, we can also ask clients "What emotion would you rather have?" and explore the actions which might constitute that preferred emotion so that it can be created from the component actions. Instead of "anxious," a client might prefer "secure" and by exploring the actions associated with security, those actions become available, and frequently lead to the desired emotion being generated.

O'Hanlon (1989) writes of his accidental discovery of the value of actions in his assisting a woman to overcome her depression when she recounted the actions she had taken to overcome the problem previously – telephoning a friend, riding her bicycle, continuing her regular activities – and in recounting them to Bill, reminded herself of the action she was not taking, and now could. The depression lifted as they spoke, and she continued in good form at follow up.

Moods And The Body

When particular emotions have been around for a time, they can seem to move in, and make themselves at home, however unwelcome they may be as guests. When this occurs, the body can change to accommodate them. If a client began to have an emotion of fear, as a response to a specific event, such as a rough plane trip, or a humiliating classroom criticism, there can be a readily recognised stooping of the shoulders, widening of the eyes, smallness of the steps when walking, so that even though the original experience may be forgotten, the memory lingers bodily.

We have all made observations of "body language," but following Maturana and languaging and then emotioning, we can explore "embodying." As with the emotional field, where we could ask about how a client would rather feel, and so assist them to access that emotion though the constitutive actions, we can also ask a client to place their body in a position, or move their body in a manner which would support or enable a preferred way of being.

If a client has poor self esteem, I frequently invite such a person to stand on my desk, placing their feet a little apart, shoulders straight, head high, stretch out their arms and say "This is Me. This is who I am." The response can be dramatic, and can forward the therapy so beautifully.

Depression, which is being promoted as the next epidemic, due to some hypothetical imbalance of brain chemistry, can more usefully be regarded as an embodied mood, frequently of resignation, hopelessness, helplessness or overloaded. Inviting a shift in body position, a lifting of the direction of the gaze, an increase in the pace of walking can allow for a delightful reconnection of the client with their partly forgotten body memories of being more fully themselves, and facilitate therapeutic progress. This can assist a client with depression to have some influence on their own experience, become more self-reliant, self-authoring – all relevant to enhancing a more desired mood, rather than encouraging dependence on some magic pill, as if such could ever exist.

A businessman wondered about resuming Prozac. Business was booming, but he was feeling overloaded, and was not attending to projects, placing his company in jeopardy. I took him for a brisk walk outside, and asked him to recount his dilemma. He was puzzled to discover that the words wouldn't come, and he experienced relief. When we continued the session inside, his mood was sufficiently changed for him to begin to move into action, and he continues to prosper, without the "miracle help" of Prozac.

A single conversation involving "How would you rather feel?" or a brisk walk is rarely enough to totally deal with a problem, but viewing emotions and the body from this action perspective can offer us and clients additional sets of observations, additional interventions, additional actions, which is always useful in our ongoing effectiveness and learning.

References:

Cade, B. & O'Hanlon, W. H., (1993) pp 42 – 48, *A Brief Guide to Brief Therapy.* WW Norton New York.

McNeilly, R. B., (2000), *Healing the Whole Person – A Solution-Focused Approach to Using Empowering Language, Emotions, and Action in Therapy.* John Wiley & Sons, New York

O'Hanlon, W. H. & Weiner-David, M, (1989) p 3, *In Search of Solutions – a New Direction in Psychotherapy* WW Norton New York

Ethics – An Evolution

Ethics will be a central concern for any human endeavour, and perhaps particularly those dealing with people and their concerns, their problems, their lives. But when we look at ethics we find a number of different approaches and like in many distinctions, ethics, and ethical concerns are not isolated phenomena. They change in a flow that is timely and coherent with the general social drift.

Minimal Standards To Belong To A Club
In the Oxford Dictionary the first definition of ethics is concerned with the rules of belonging to a club. Here the concern is about what are the minimal standards, the minimal requirements to belong to a club. Ethics committees concern themselves with someone doing something unethical, so in the maintenance of minimal standards they are not concerned so much about ethics as the lack of it. If someone does not abide by the rules they get thrown out of the club. If someone doesn't meet the minimal standards they are expelled from that community.

This basic fundamental notion within this definition of ethics is concerned with belonging. If you want to be a member of the APS there are certain things that you have to do. If a Doctor does something they shouldn't do, they can expect an ethical inquiry. I had a letter sent to me by the Medical Board ten years ago when someone wrote an article about what I was doing in the newspaper because the Board was very sensitive about advertising at that stage and they wanted to know if I approached the journalist or if they approached me. If I had approached them that would of been advertising and I could have been fined or rebuked - it would have been unethical.

Towards Excellence

Another definition in the Oxford Dictionary is not about minimal standards but is about human duty in its widest extent. This invites an ethical approach to working in clinical circumstances to attend to what can we do to contribute maximally to a client, what can we do that is in their best interest. This shifts the focus from minimal standards to a concern about excellence, and it brings a very different mood. It's not about doing the least to stay safe, but rather how to be most useful.

Increasing Options

Heinz von Foerster stated what he called the ethical imperative, he was talking not only about therapy but life in general as being to increase options. We have often said in our work that we want to try to increase the options for our clients and it makes sense because problems have fewer options, solutions are characterised by a range of options, so it makes sense clinically to increase options but von Foerster is saying that this is an ethical issue. He says we have an ethical imperative to increase options for our clients, in education and in our family.

Learning To Live Together

Humberto Maturana claims, as a biologist that love is the fundamental human social emotion and to have a biologist that thinks this way is interesting. By love he doesn't mean sentimentality or being in love. He takes love as an extension of respect, and he says that love is an emotion in which we grant legitimacy to another person to live in the world beside us. This extends to another creature - a spider or a tree, so love for Maturana is a matter of the legitimacy of another so we can live with them.

He says that learning to live together is the prime human ethic, and I think this has become the most pressing contemporary issue that our ethics needs to address. The world that we are in, the world of the Internet, cyberspace, international travel is changing at an escalating rate. One Thursday I was in Melbourne and the next Thursday I was in Melbourne again having been in a different country where people had come from Venezuela, from Chile, from Mexico as well as Philadelphia and all over the US as well as from Australia. These people from different countries, with different languages, different backgrounds, different cultures, different histories and yet we were working together, and this kind of experience is increasingly common. It was superb.

Whenever we don't learn to work together, to live peacefully together, we have conflict. We saw an example of that in the recent waterfront dispute. Whenever people dig in about standards there's war. When a group of people who hold a fundamentalist belief that their standards are the right standards, "my way is the right way and your way is the wrong way," and the other side said "no my way is the right way and your way is the wrong way" - there's conflict and enmity.

I heard on radio this morning where there are some Second World War Veterans in Britain that are furious that the Queen is wanting to award the Japanese Emperor The Order of The Garter because they are saying the Japanese Emperor caused of a lot of trouble in the Second World War so how could he be given the Order of The Garter? He doesn't belong to that club, he should be excluded. But if we see that we are wanting to live in a world which is shrinking we have to live with people who were enemies. We have to otherwise we will keep fighting.

The issue of living together is not just a matter of being nice to each other, but it's an ethical issue. In Chile terrible things happened with torture, imprisonment, but I understand they are saying "That's past." They are actually saying that they have to learn to put all that enmity in the past so that the previous torturers and torturees are now talking to each other. They are not wanting reparations. They are not wanting anything. They are saying they have got to get on with the task of working together.

Our world is a shrinking, mobile, multicultural community with increasing complexity. We can't avoid it. We can no longer say that my way is right and your way is wrong. If we look at the controversy in Europe about the Euro, where some countries are saying this is going to be to their detriment. If they give up their currency it may hurt them financially, but Europe is moving towards a new kind of community which demands living together.

In our clinical work, the mood and the concerns that we are attending to invite us to give less attention to what is the right way to do things, what is the right way for client to respond, and more attention to what can do or that they can do to solve their problems. We want to increase their options but underpinning all of that is the concern, how can we work effectively with this client.

I think that living together is an issue that we need to put in an ethical domain - an ethical concern with practical repercussions. When I look and see this ethical shift from rules and towards living together I see it paralleling a social change. Previous eras were concerned with the minimal rules required to remain in a club, with worries about control, maintaining power in a hierarchy, giving authority to someone who could say your in or your out. Living together these days we don't have the choice of "your in," "your out." We're all in this soup together.

I haven't previously spoken about ethics as a focus because it seemed to me to be better to show it rather than to speak about it. When we're working together where actually in this, we're doing this. One of my joys of this work is to see how a group of individuals come together at the beginning of a program and by the end of it we're living together, sharing, learning things we didn't know before.

For me this is ethics at its best.

"Every human act takes place in language. Every act in language brings forth a world created with others in the act of coexistence which gives rise to what is human. Thus every human act has an ethical meaning because it is an act of constitution of the human world. The linkage of human to human is, in the final analysis, the groundwork of all ethics as a reflection on the legitimacy of the presence of others." Humberto Maturana in "Tree of Know-ledge" p 247.

Hypnosis, Dissociation And Spontaneous Trance: Erickson's Contribution

Students and practitioners of hypnosis learn trance inductions and phenomena as a new and often strange process. Erickson's observational approach allows for a naturalistic and nonintrusive experience for the hypnotic client. This emphasis on the naturalness of hypnosis allows for a readily useful integration of the therapy and at the same time promotes a sense of autonomy in the client thus avoiding the power issue, which seems to have haunted the hypnotic scene. Erickson emphasised the "common every - day trance" with examples of spontaneous catalepsy, dissociation and other trance experiences, inviting the client to explore their own individual abilities which then become available for the therapeutic process. This paper investigates how this approach can empower therapist and client to find the most effective solution to the problem. It will address how we as students can learn from Erickson's work without being lost in the "mystical" methods he was so famous for. Working in this way allows both client and therapist to co-operate so that there is a sense of ease and naturalness. This permits the therapy to be integrated readily and securely.

Hypnosis, dissociation and spontaneous trance are common everyday experiences and Erickson alerted us to this in such a way that these experiences can be incorporated in the therapeutic process as it evolves.

As you sit, listening or reading, an altered state of awareness is probably already beginning simply by doing that there is an alteration of perception of for example the sensations of feet on the floor, hands in the lap or wherever they are, breathing in and out, watch on the wrist, glasses on the nose etc. All these sensations are able to be attended to, to an increased or decreased degree or not at all. Some may already have begun to allow this experience to begin to be in the background so that other thoughts, relevant or irrelevant can be attended to. The words are audible or readable but we have all had a lot of experience in not hearing such sounds or not seeing such words.

This could be the beginning of an experience of dissociation.

How many people are at this time unaware of the way time seems to be passing so quickly or is it dragging? Who could doubt the readiness to not notice how something which happened just a few moments ago has already been forgotten? A word a sound a thought a sensation such as an itch or sense of comfort a mood such as boredom or interest or fascination. All these can be present and even noticed and then naturally give way to the next experience.

Sitting listening or reading and attending or not attending, it is very likely that changes in pulse rate, lowering of blood pressure, alteration of blinking and swallowing reflexes and other physiological variables have already begun. So too, relaxation of various muscles such as those of the face and neck, a change in the circulation in the skin so that there may be a degree of pallor of the face or perhaps some flushing. It is not unlikely that there are areas of actual numbness whether noticed or not.

The classical trance experiences such as time distortion, amnesia, alteration of physiological function can be seen to be an extension of such familiar, everyday experiences. Erickson and Rossi suggest (Hypnotic Realities p71) that all hypnosis can be thought of as dissociative. "We may hypothesise that in general a hypnotic phenomenon takes place imply by dissociating any behaviour from it's usual associational context … catalepsy can be evoked by dissociating the ability to move a part of the body from … wakening: anesthesia by dissociating the ability to feel: amnesia … to remember.

The classical hypnotic phenomena of age regression, automatic writing, hallucinations and time distortion can be understood as "normal" aspects of behaviour that take place in an autonomous or hypnotic manner simply by separating them from their usual associational contexts."

It is observations such as these which Erickson alerted us to and so these naturally occurring experiences can allow the therapist to lead the client to extend these into what we may recognise as trance. This in such a way that since the original experience is the client's the development is likely to be accepted by the client and become a natural part of the client's own experience to be accessed in the usual way that the client could access other resources originating and developing in the client.

Should it be judged that the resource that the client requires to deal with a problem - say anxiety about flying - is to learn to dissociate from the problem response - anxiety - and re-associate with a response of security or trust, then the trance induction could begin by the therapist noticing moments when spontaneous dissociation can be observed and help the client to build on those. The therapist could notice and encourage any tendency in the client to gaze into the distance, to not need to attend to the stimuli external to the client, to become less interested in the body sensations such as feet on the floor, back on the chair, hands on the lap, etc. and more interested in the experience of becoming increasingly absorbed by various other experiences such as remembering how it feels in the body to be safe and secure, in the thinking to remember times when that experience was vividly present, in reflecting on how behaviours change, past difficulties have already been overcome.

Learning to walk which often began so haltingly is now for most a natural and secure learning. Learning to write which began with a sense of being overwhelmed by all those letters is now an automatic skill which couldn't be forgotten even with conscious effort.

Learning to ride a bicycle which was accompanied by bruises and grazes can now be something which has already been extended for many into other learning's such as driving a car.

Speculation about the security of those changes can lead to a willingness to speculate about other secure changes including the therapeutic change already begun.

In this way the client is lead to explore their own experience and resources so that they naturally fit and remain secure within the client. By inviting this individual client to explore their own experience, there are additional options provided and hence a greater sense of autonomy which is then likely to be empowering to the client, leaving them with the expectation of being more able to deal with similar or different difficulties in the future.

A client with a pain problem may want to learn how to be more comfortable. It can be so helpful in helping the client to learn to deal more effectively with their experience to know that although the pain is real and at times distressing, that there are ways that any person has in which that expectation can change.

A dramatic example from Erickson's work is the case of a woman suffering severe pain from terminal cancer. He let her know that he was very aware of the severity of her pain, her helplessness in the face of the pain and then in a dramatic manner distracted her (producing the dissociation which is characteristic of a surprise) and allowed her to learn a new way of processing her experience. He said that he could see that she was in severe pain and that she wanted to get rid of the pain but didn't as yet know how to do that. He then said that if that door there were to open and you were to see in the doorway a large hungry tiger, drooling at the mouth and looking straight at you, how much pain do you think you would feel to which she replied that she didn't feel any pain just thinking about it and

that she would take the tiger back to the hospital and keep it under the bed so that it would be there any time she needed it. And it was HER tiger, not Erickson's and it was for HER to use whenever SHE wanted.

A woman wanting to learn to use hypnosis to have a comfortable and satisfying delivery of her baby may be invited to enjoy the experience of not needing to notice a lot of sensations she could notice in her body right now to not notice as various sounds around including the sound of my voice can begin to fade into the background of her experience they can nevertheless in some way add to her experience of comfort and well-being so that she can begin to attend to something much more relevant and interesting to her such as the experience of looking forward to holding her child. She might enjoy wondering will it be a boy or a girl, will it have long hair or short, dark or fair or perhaps none at all, will it look like her or the father? There may be many other questions she may have and be naturally interested to wonder about. While she is doing this she may or may not notice how even though time passes without her needing to pay particular attention to it, her breathing in and out naturally adds to her sense of increasing comfort and control, and that really her body knows much better than she does about how to allow the natural process of childbirth to take its own course. So why not just lie back and let the process develop with an ever increasing willingness to enjoy the way she really has a lot of skills and strengths she is about to find out so that she can expect to take these skills and strengths into her relationship with the child as it grows and develops.

Mesmer thought that the source of the hypnotic experience was in him - he had THE POWER. His ghost may be heard as you pass not by that billabong, but in any hypnotic interaction where the hypnotist takes a position of power in relation to the presumed less powerful client, forgetting that Erickson alerted us to looking to the client as the source of their own potential power so that the therapist's work is to assist the client to tap into their own source of powerful resources.

Erickson said that all he did was to practice simple common sense psychology and by utilising the experience of spontaneous trance, dissociation already present in the client, hypnosis and the various hypnotic phenomena can be revealed and incorporated, permitting the therapy to be integrated readily and securely. This allows students and practitioners of hypnosis to learn trance inductions and phenomena in an already familiar way.

This invitation was Erickson's contribution to hypnosis, dissociation and spontaneous trance.

Learning To Learn

Learning Therapy

Problems are the substance of therapy; the reason people seek it out, or Counselling. They are also the substance of living and are a result of an interruption of a transparency or the smooth flowing of events, when life is going well. Response to change is of the essence here. Change asks for adaption, or learning, as we tend to assess these changes negatively. If we assume that problems are a resisting of learning or a blindness to the specific learning, or to learning itself or where the sufferer assesses that the learning required is beyond their capacity, some interesting and useful possibilities appear. One way of not learning, not adapting is by avoidance. Avoiding learning can be achieved by some sort of dissociation from the experience, which results in avoiding the invitation to learn which the experience calls us to. Every day trances, obsessive behaviour, drug abuse, fundamentalist beliefs and any rigidity are all relevant.

Avoiding learning follows an assumption that one already possesses the truth, the way, the answer, so one remains right in the face of a world experience which deviates from some ideal, and which assumes that to go along with the changes one faces would betray one's beliefs. Solving a problem by adapting and learning then creates an even worse problem - this time a moral or ethical one. The solution then becomes the problem, while the problem is the solution in that as long as the problem remains, one's moral or ethical stand is in place. Calvinism is right here, and can advocate keeping the problem as noble suffering and solving it as surrendering to the ways of the devil, the flesh, the world, or something definitely evil and to be avoided. Fear is the predominant emotion.

Another way we can avoid learning is to not recognise the problem as problematic – to be blind to it or to be resigned to our inability to deal with it.

We could define a problem then as some difficulty experienced in learning to cope with a change. This definition is only one of many, and is offered as one way of designing interventions. I like it because it invites anyone's suffering into the space of normality, and learning. It follows then that any problem, whatever its form or magnitude can then be viewed as an invitation to learning. Some invitations will be soft, others imperative. Curiosity is the predominant emotion.

Some learning require the application of something previously learnt in another area of experience, while some will require learning something new. In the former, we can think of a problem as a circumstance in which a specific resource is not being utilised, that if it were, there would be no problem, and which is being utilised in another area of the client's life which is not problematic. If the latter, then we can ask "how have you learnt previously?" Or " how do you prefer to learn?" So setting up the conversation of learning this new requirement based on past learning's - learning to learn.

Erickson spoke of curiosity, early learning as a child of crawling, walking, writing, etc., and said that "all our lives we are learning."

Learning requires a mood of uncertainty, possibility, and trust. "Trust your unconscious." Without learning we are condemned to surviving - to endlessly repeating a loop of past behaviour, locked into some previous way of being or doing. With learning comes the opportunity to explore, wonder, adapt, experience liveliness, joy, passion, and lots of other benefits.

Therapy can then be transformed into assisting someone to learn. Learning to be a therapist then requires learning to facilitate learning in others. Teaching therapists becomes facilitating someone to facilitate someone to facilitate their own experience and so learning to experience facilitation. How different this is from attempting to fix some defective person or transmit information or knowledge or some pre-packaged method!

Therapists would then need to learn to generate a mood, which would foster learning in their client, and teachers of therapists in their students. This invites a watchful expectant respect for the client, and demands a putting aside of any of the student's certainties, prejudices, opinions, and expectations. It's not so much a matter of learning how to be, but rather how to not be; not so much what to do, but what to not do. "Who can remain still until the moment of action?" Lao Tzu and also invites a shift of focus from human being to human becoming.

When some circumstance happens, we can experience it as it is with peaceful acceptance; we can have it be a dilemma where it is accepted as less than ideal, but a solution is not immediately required; we can have it be a problem thereby requiring a solution; or we can even wonder about the opportunity this circumstance might bring.

What happens to transform a problem into a dilemma into an experience into an opportunity?

A problem has no available relevant actions; a dilemma has possible actions which are at the time not requiring action; an experience has no concern for action; an opportunity is action waiting to happen and each happen in different moods - from acceptance, through curiosity, suffering and wonder.

Learning Sensitivity
Linking learning to therapy brings certain concerns including what is learning and how we can facilitate learning. How we are relating to learning is changing. Until recently, we thought of knowing as acquiring information, arranging or computing that information to create an understanding or a model of understanding which we could then act on - something like making a map of an area of country and then using the map to find our way around.

We can appreciate learning as an assessment made about differential capabilities occurring over time. If at one time we are not able to perform a particular action, and at a later time we are able to, we say that learning has occurred. It is crucial to distinguish education from training here. Education – from the Latin "educare" – "to draw out" is very different from the imparting of information requiring that it be taken in, or training which requires a different predetermined behaviour. Imparting information and training require a passivity by the student, and bring a mood of fear with a concern for control. Education is a creative experience requiring active participation by the student, and brings a mood of legitimacy, curiosity, and openness.

The map maker would be expected to get to know the area, to wander around in it, not necessarily knowing what he was looking for, and then beginning to notice certain patterns – hills, rivers, flats for cultivation, etc. The value of the map is that it allows those who follow to go more directly or to look with specific concerns in mind, and avoid the need for repetitive exploration with its necessary blind alleys, false hunches, mistakes, etc.

Once the map user begins to use the map, they soon stop referring to it, and begin to find their own way around, perhaps referring to the map from time to time if they are uncertain or wish to explore something different.

The map becomes less and less important, except for historical interest, and then travelling becomes transparent, automatic, outside of awareness, habitual.

Captain Cook discovered Botany Bay and wrote glowingly about its potential and only noticed Port Jackson as he sailed past it. Although his judgments subsequently were seen to be incorrect, his mapping of the East coast of Australia made future exploration possible by serving as a starting point for future map makers.

When we move into a different house, we begin to discover which room is which; where to sleep, where's the bathroom, toilet, kitchen, etc. Later in the day, we begin to explore light switches, power points, and door locks. Still later, we might look for a switch board, a tap to turn off the water at the mains, the hot water system. As we continue to live in this house, we begin to discover more about the house, and also more about what is to be discovered that we didn't even think to look for at first – perhaps an extra storage cupboard we overlooked at first, perhaps a rose that comes into bloom that we previously overlooked. We may also discover tasks to attend to – squeaky hinges, badly fitting doors, weeds in the garden – none of which were apparent when we first moved in. We may even rearrange the rooms, repaint them, perhaps even pull down a wall, or extend the house. Living in this new house allows us to become more sensitive to the house as we are in the experience of living in it.

There is a crisis in learning at this time in our history, due in part to the assumption that learning is linked with information, and dissatisfaction, frustration, and resignation are part of the "education" system from primary through to post-tertiary.

These problem-generating approaches allow for coping or managing situations, but unwittingly preclude moving beyond them. Learning as we are exploring allows the possibility of moving past or beyond a situation and creating a different preferred experience.

A generation ago we went to school or university, learnt skills and then went to work to apply those skills. With the escalation of the new technologies this is no longer adequate. We are now faced with the imperative of learning as an ongoing lifetime activity, with recurrent revising previous ideas which were "known" and are now seen as redundant. A concern with learning has now been transformed into a concern with learning to learn – to give attention to the learning process itself.

When we are learning a new approach to therapy, such as hypnosis, we can put ourselves in the experience, not knowing what we should be looking for, not knowing what to ask, what to say, how to respond, and yet as the process continues, we begin to discover, each individually, how to find our way round this new territory.

Wittgenstein wrote: "My propositions are elucidatory in this way: he who understands me finally recognises them as senseless, when he has climbed out through them, on them, over them. (He must so to speak throw away the ladder, after he has climbed up on it.) He must surmount these propositions; then he sees the world rightly. Whereof one cannot speak, thereof one must remain silent."

The one map maker could make many different maps of the same area – topography, soil types, vegetation – for different map users – builders, gardeners, farmers – but the process of map making involves making distinctions or creating ways of referring to the area which would have already become transparent to the map maker.

What is the process for the mapmaker, before he makes the map? How does he get to know the area so that he can begin to map it – not just in one way, but also in a variety of ways? In our everyday speaking we would say that he gets to know the area, becomes familiar with it, experiences it, gets used to it. In this inquiry I am going to use the notion of "sensitivity" as used by Spinosa, Flores and Dreyfus in "Disclosing New Worlds" (p39) - "This book, then, is attempting to develop sensitivities, not knowledge. Once one has a sensitivity to something such as food, decency, certain kinds of beauty, or even the pleasure of hiking, one is already on the path of refining and developing that sensitivity. One sees food, decent behaviour, beauty, and hiking trails in a new light. They draw one to them in a way they did not before. As one is drawn, time and time again, one then continuously develops one's skills for dealing with what one is sensitive to."

We could say that the mapmaker learns the area by becoming sensitive to it over time and recurrent experience, each recurrent experience allowing for increased or new sensitivities – increased sensitivity in the ways of observing what has already been created and new sensitivities as a result of new ways of observing that might suddenly appear – as if from nowhere. In looking for the direction of river flow and steepness of land for grazing or crop cultivation, the map maker might notice tall, straight trees which could be used for house construction, or a new kind or bird or animal which could create the possibility for research or tourism.

The experience of becoming sensitive can also allow an increasing sensitivity to the process of being sensitive itself. As we develop more sensitivity to a particular way of observing, we begin to sense more ways of observing, and so on.

We can now say that learning, becoming more competent, finding our own way around some area – either physical or intellectual such as therapy – can be approached with the questions – "What would be useful for me to develop sensitivity to?" And "How could we develop these sensitivities?"

We know from our everyday experience that if we want to learn something like riding a bike, another language or computer program, that we get on the bike, into conversations in the new language, or in front of the computer and begin to "play." This translates into any area of learning and invites us to get into the soup of whatever we are wanting to learn.

Our everyday experience also teaches us that early on we will make many mistakes – fall off the bike, say the wrong foreign word, press the wrong computer key – and that making these mistakes provides us with the actual experience of learning what we are wanting to learn.

Learning For The Observer

This process can begin as an interruption to our automatic activity – and we find ourselves being uncertain, not knowing what to do, where to go, what to say. We can recognise that we didn't know what to do, and ask for another to teach us. This will happen if the issue is important to us, if something is missing for us and may include a willingness to open or soften to learning, perhaps observing others more skilled in this particular area, with a willingness to allow time and learning plateaus to happen.

Listening, curiosity are central here so the observer we are, our way of observing, can undergo a change, can learn, so we can again let self awareness rest in the background of our experience as a new transparency evolves. It can be helpful to reflect on what will facilitate this process, what can usefully be cleared out of the way so that we can be more "in touch with ourselves," more centered, more together, less reactive, more available, more transparent.

Learning To Learn

We are claiming that problems are rooted in lack of adaption to change, i.e. lack of learning, and that therapy is concerned with providing opportunities to learn. It is then of central concern to observe ongoingly what skills our clients may demonstrate in learning, and what additional assistance they may require to learn what they need to learn.

Oftentimes the therapy IS finding the area of learning to be explored. "If you don't know where you are going, you might end up in a different place." Once the area of learning is defined, the conversation can help to recall previous learning's, or previous attitudes to learning which can then allow the learning to proceed, and the solution to emerge.

Every human is blind to some area of experience. If this blindness interferes with our functioning, we experience a problem. Problems can be resolved by recognising these areas of blindness, so we can literally begin to see or distinguish what was previously transparent. We can only intervene in a world we can see.

If we ask "How do you learn best?" Or "What has helped you to learn previously?" Or "What has the experience of learning been like for you when it has happened best?" This can lead directly to the **experience** of learning which will be useful for this client or our self. We may be told that it's like playing, being curious, copying another, soaking up an experience, or even being present without any agenda, engaged, interested, passively waiting to be surprised in a mood of wonderment.

Identifying some blocks or impediments to learning allows us to ask "What's missing?" And deal with those difficulties – to learn what will help us to move beyond them.

Julio Olalla and Rafael Echeverria from the Newfield Group's MAPC commented on what they called enemies of learning and the following list of allies of learning derives directly from their ideas.

1)   Ability to admit ignorance (ignorance is a high state of knowing).

2)   I can't fully know. This occurs in a mood of humility.

3)   Awareness of blindness (cognitive blindness) - I know that I don't know.

4)   I can't be clear about things all the time.

5)   Remembering the embodying of learning through repetition or experience.

6)   Putting aside of significance or self importance.

7)   Seriousness (without heaviness).

8)   Granting permission to be taught.

9)   Putting assessing aside.

10)   Learning is possible, given who I am.

11)   Separating opinions from knowledge.

12)   Separating information from knowing.

13)   Making time.

14)   Openness to mistakes and trust.

15)   Questioning our questions.

16)   Distinguishing knowing from having the truth.

Often a mood of fear is identified with an assessment of lack of trust in the background.

When we ask "What's missing?" We will see variations of the answers to asking about when learning went well. If trust is missing, and in my experience self-trust is always in question in any problem situation, then we can invite a prudent exploration of the possibility of learning to regain trust – again we find our self in the experience of learning. Other issues which may emerge may include humility if arrogance is what blocking learning; or confidence if wariness of criticisms by others was problematic.

Maturana said that learning is an emotion, not a matter of information. He said that learning begins when the student takes the hand of the teacher. For this to happen, trust is a prerequisite, and instead of naively hoping, thus inviting betrayal, trust can emerge again, through an experience of learning. In this circularity, prudence brings with it the possibility of relearning to trust in a grounded, solid, manageable way.

Summary
If therapy is concerned with problems and if we link problems with an invitation to learn, then therapy can be regarded as an opportunity to facilitate learning in the client and invites us to examine and develop our own learning process to avoid potential barriers and facilitate its evolution. Our learning to learn can then encourage our clients' learning and even their own learning about learning so they can then be best prepared for the vicissitudes and unpredictable experiences which

constitute life and enhance their and our living fully and satisfyingly.

Psychotherapy In The Drift Of Social History Time, Pace And Power

Psychotherapy happens in a culture, at a time in history, and is influenced, perhaps is even an expression of that culture. How therapy was 100 years ago, 50 years ago differs from how therapy is now, and again from how it will be in 10, 20, 50 years time. I am wanting to correlate some landmarks in the evolution of psychotherapy with the culture and time in which they occurred.

I invite you to examine, with me, how this evolution relates to time orientation, pace, and power structure. All the following comments are made as observations. None of them are intended to moralise, criticise or praise any particular aspect.

Early 1900s - Freud.
Early last century, there was a veneration of tradition in Vienna. Archeology was popular. The time orientation was very much to the past. Life moved at a gentlemanly pace, the horse and buggy were beginning to be replaced by the even slower automobile. The pace was unhurried. There were numerous empires and their kings or emperors. Patriarchy ruled in the family. The power structure was markedly hierarchical.

It is not surprising, then, that Freud's therapy was past oriented, unhurried, sometimes taking years, and the therapist was powerful. Should a client recover too rapidly, they may be diagnosed as suffering from "flight into health," thus requiring MORE, not less therapy.

Mid 1900's - Vietnam, the bomb, and Perls.
After "the bomb," at any moment someone might push the button, and we would all disintegrate as part of an explosion of nuclear particles. There was no future. The disillusionment with the Vietnam war in particular, and the establishment generally, the past was seen as irrelevant, not to be trusted. The past was gone, the future was gone. All there was, was the present.

The pace of life was quickening on the roads, in aeronautics, and telecommunication. Empires were crumbling; Emperors and Kings were replaced by egalitarianism. Parents strove to make friends with their children, to promote children to equals.

The "now generation," the "me generation" flourished, and into this milieu came Gestalt Therapy. The past was significant only as a place of unfinished business, which could be completed, and let go of. No future discussion and hence the hallmark question of Gestalt - "what's happening NOW?" (emphasis mine). Psychotherapy was shorter, and the power was shared equally. Gestalt therapists were on first name terms with their clients.

Late 1900s - Future Design.
Towards the end of the century, even the present has been rejected as unsustainable. Conservation issues influence

electoral results. We are informed that we need to design a different future if we are to survive as a species. We find ourselves forced into a future time orientation.

The pace of our society is accelerating - in travel, computers, and telecommunications. We want immediate service if our phone line is out of order, or if our car breaks down. Adaptability and responsiveness are the emerging creed of business.

The power structure is now the reverse of the early 1900s. Our children tell us what they will or more often will not do. Business is increasingly obsessed with "customer satisfaction." Factory workers are active in company policy design. New international alliances are being forged.

So, not surprisingly, psychotherapy is increasingly future oriented, is increasingly brief in duration, and the therapist is likely to ask something like "what would you like to achieve here?" The power is with the client, not the trained professional.

After 2000 - accountability & cyber-life.
Accountability is the catch cry of the moment. Schools, universities, the medical profession, and therapists are now expected to be accountable. Teachers complain that they spend so much time filling out assessments about their students that they have little time to teach. Universities have become multi-million dollar businesses that are required to be financially accountable. Intensive care nurses complain that they are so

busy filling out accountability forms that they have little time to attend to their patients. Managed care companies required therapists to spend up to one third of their time filling our forms.

All of these measures can be seen as a further loss of power, and George Orwell might have a wry response. Education, medicine, and therapy have all been colonised by accountants - bureaucrats who know nothing about learning, health or human dilemmas.

The internet has also inserted itself into our lives at many levels. We shop on eBay or Amazon, we read journals and the daily news on line; and communicate with Facebook: people find business and life partners on-line.

So, given this obsession with accountability, no wonder Scott Miller and friends' ORS and SRS measures are gaining acceptance. And, given the Internet juggernaut, no wonder there is an increase in on-line learning and Internet Counselling.

Where to from here?
It is fascinating to speculate how psychotherapy will continue to develop, as change and develop it will undoubtedly. Will it become even more technology driven? Will each computer have a built in programmed to provide therapy for the uncertain owner? Or will there be a full turn of the wheel, and perhaps "old-fashioned" values will return. Will there be a neo-human

interaction session, with revisiting present or even past experiences?

No-one can predict accurately just what direction psychotherapy will take, but it seems valuable to be able to observe the direction society in general is taking, so we can continue to design and provide therapy which will be relevant.

We can also speculate about what themes have been conserved throughout all these changes. With the social evolving's, what principles, concerns, interactions have been maintained as a thread around which all the changes have happened.

Recognising the current trends can allow us to learn the steps of this dance, which can allow us to maintain out dignity and personal integrity while living peacefully in the "real world" of popular culture.

About Nothing

"Wominjeka Yearmenn Bunjilaka"

Welcome to Bunjilaka (Wominjeka is a Woiwurrung language word meaning welcome).

What is Bunjilaka? Bunjilaka is the Aboriginal Centre at Melbourne Museum in Carlton Gardens just north of Melbourne's Central Business District.

The name Bunjilaka is derived from the word 'Bunjil' (Woiwurung language) who was a significant Creation Ancestor for some southeastern Aboriginal language groups, and 'Aka', (Boonwurung language) meaning land or place. The name was selected after consultation with the local Aboriginal people from the Wurundjeri and Boonwurung groups who are the traditional owners of the Melbourne and surrounding suburbs. The words evoke the sense of a "creation place," which suits the functions Bunjilaka staff and Indigenous Cultures Program staff wish to achieve."

This invitation seemed so fitting, bringing our attention to *creation*.

Creation requires that we begin with nothing - anything else is mere rearrangement. We can only create a new house if we first clear the block or we are renovating. We can only create a new document if we begin with a blank page, otherwise we are editing.

One of the key characteristics of the Ericksonian approach is creativity – to get past any preconceptions of how a client *should* be, change, respond, and be open to them as they are. One therapeutic option is to begin with some formulation, diagnostic schema, or preplanned treatment and apply it – a rearrangement of the client (always for their benefit, but from the wisdom and power of the therapist). Erickson invited us into another approach - to give the client as much opportunity as possible to explore their own experience, their own resources, their own goals. This process is creative and requires that we remove anything in the way, so there is then *nothing* in our way of assisting the client to achieve their experience of having *nothing* preventing them from becoming how they wish, or perhaps really are.

In 1984 I was completing a personal development programme called "The EST Training" and was one of 150 or so people sitting with my eyes closed, following instructions and imagining that the person on either side of me was dangerous to me, then 2 then 4, then 10 people on either side of me were dangerous to me, then the whole room, then the whole of Melbourne, then Australia, then the world. It was a truly terrifying experience. Then the process changed. If a person on either side of me was dangerous to me, I must be dangerous to the people on either side of me. If 2, 4, 10 were dangerous to me, I must be dangerous to these 2, 4, 10. This extended to the room,

Melbourne, Australia, the world. The whole world was frightened of me. At some point, the terror transformed itself into the greatest joke of my life, and the total absurdity remains with me to this day, and continues to tickle my experience just by me remembering it.

How could terror transform into absurdity? There must have been a pivotal point – a *nothing* point. But how can we get to that point of transformation?

Lao Tzu wrote 2 ½ thousand years ago in #11 of his
Tao Te Ching:

> "Thirty spokes share the wheel's hub;
> It is the centre hole that makes it useful.
> Shape clay into a vessel;
> It is the space within that makes it useful.
> Cut doors and windows for a room;
> It is the holes which make it useful.
> Therefore profit comes from what is there;
> Usefulness from what is not there."

Listening is one of the fundamental acts, if not the fundamental act of the solution oriented approach. When we assume that clients have resources, and only experience problems when disconnected from these resources or their resourcefulness, we will naturally want to listen *for* what resources may be missing in their problem experience, where these resources may already be present in their functioning life, how this particular individual connects experiences, learns experiences, embodies experiences.

All these processes involve listening to the particular client rather to some theory, or our own ideas of what might be helpful.

Scott Miller, Barry Duncan & Jaqueline Sparks ("The Myth of the Magic Pill" Psychotherapy in Australia Vol 6 no 3 May 2000) write about the importance of listening to the client's experience, their stories, their goals to form a strong therapeutic relationship. Michael Lambert's 1992 research is quoted in The Family Therapy Networker July/August 1997 by Barry Duncan, Mark Hubble & Scott Miller "Stepping off the Throne" p27 & 28, in which client factors were responsible for 40% of clients' improvement, therapeutic alliance for 30%, and technique for a mere 15%. This adds further weight to the importance of listening to the client.

We can know about this, but are so easily seduced into listening to our own thoughts, ideas, plans, outcomes, that we can become deaf to the client's experience. The temptation, then, can be to label the client as difficult, resistant, having secondary gain, etc., instead of recognising our own rigidities. Letting these go, while a challenge, can be so rewarding for both sides of the conversation, and *nothing* is again the issue here.

We have all learnt this, so why is it so difficult, or even near to impossible at times? A colleague reported feeling uncomfortable, saying she felt I was "teaching at her" in a conversation. Her comments had the effect of quieting my thoughts about what *should* be happening, and the resulting space, or *nothing*, opened my seeing of her so she actually appeared out of the blur I had unwittingly created. In getting to *nothing* I could put aside my projections, so we could begin to create a useful and relevant interaction together.

How often do our clients tolerate us not listening, hoping that one day, someone, anyone, *ANYONE* might see them, hear them, recognise them?

This brings the question "How can we listen to a client, when we are attuned to listening to our own thoughts about the client?" and invites exploration of quieting, if not silencing our thoughts, or perhaps loosening our attachment to them. How can we get to *nothing*?

When I read Lao Tzu, chapter 56 of Tao Te Ching: "Those that know do not talk. Those that talk do not know" I was reminded of Erickson's invitation to "observe, observe, observe." How can we actually achieve this? How can ensure that our thinking and speaking doesn't interfere with our listening to our client? Perhaps sometimes silence?

Various writers have commented about this issue. The entry for January 14th in The Dalai Lama's Book of Daily meditations is: "Sometimes one creates a dynamic impression by saying something. And sometimes one creates as significant an impression by remaining silent." Wittgenstein's words "Whereof one cannot speak, thereof one should pass in silence," while they invite silence, also hint, to me, at a respectful listening without trying to explain, and in a mood of wonder and acceptance. Lao Tzu again points to this in chapter 64 of Tao Te Ching: "Knowing nothing needs to be done is the place we begin to move from" and this doesn't necessarily mean we should sit paralysed, but rather to avoid pushing the river, and merely take action to remove obstacles so there is then *nothing* in the way of the natural flow. From Lao Tzu again in chapter 32, "Tao in the world is like a river flowing home to the sea."

Sue-Ann Post wrote in the Today section of The Age, page 1, 10.11.2000, "I reckon my cats do absolutely nothing 90 per cent of the time. Now that's what I call a role model." With the frantic pace of contemporary life, we all want to learn from such a wise animal.

Erickson's invitation into hypnosis might include "You don't need to listen to me. You don't need to attend to my words. You don't even need to keep your eyes open, but you can close them NOW" and is echoed by Joseph Barber's soothing suggestion "With *nothing* to bother and *nothing* to disturb."

Previously, I explored my appreciation of Heidegger's listening from the clearing which, by finding ways to connect, blend, meld, merge with the other (person, forest, experience), allows us to experience *nothing* separating us, no boundaries, and permits an immediate gateway into the spiritual realm to appear. For me, this is the place to listen from, a place where listening becomes possible.

But there's always *something*. This has even become a cliché. If it's not the gas bill, it's the car registration. If it's not the cleaning, it's the painting, if it's not the lawn; it's the garden – always *something* in the way of the *nothing* that we seek.

Also we humans are so intriguingly ambivalent. We can hang out for a holiday, and when it happens, we get bored. We are desperate for THE relationship, and then find ourselves singing the line from Peggy Lee – "Is that all there is? ..."

We know the bliss of *nothing* but seem to fall into filling that *nothing* with *something*, even *anything*. Just as nature abhors a vacuum, human nature abhors the experience of *nothing*. So there is an area for learning, for exploration, for wondering that emerges from this dilemma – how can we get past the *something*, the *anything*, and experience *nothing* so that what we are seeking has at least the possibility of appearing?

A person can sit, and even though there can be sensations, there isn't really any need to attend to those sensations that don't require attention. They can be there, somewhere in the background, but they can be ignored. Even though they are there, it can be as if they aren't there at all.

A person can be reading, attending to the experience, having their own thought, making their own connections, creating their own learning, and at the same time, there is no need to count the words, recognise individual letters. They can disappear into the general experience of attending to the images, and even though there are many potential diversions, these diversions seem to disappear and the texture, the experience of the story itself can be where the attention simply finds itself.

The same person can listen to music, to the sounds of nature, to the silence of a sunset, and even though there may be other sounds, even though there may be the sounds that are there, or the silence, all this can become background, and only the important and relevant sounds or lack of sounds can be what is attended to.

It is also possible for sensations, stories, pleasurable sounds to also begin to disappear, so then a rather delightful numbness, a sense of peace, and a silence can be there, perhaps the kind of peaceful silence that we could experience if we were in the middle of outer space, or in the middle of inner space, or in the middle of nowhere, or in the middle of somewhere, without needing or even wanting to be concerned about inner or outer, somewhere or nowhere, but simply, peacefully, completely freed and immersed in the experience with nothing happening to disturb the fullness of the sense of peace and completeness.

We can look at the night sky, imagine being somewhere there, nowhere in particular, and watch the universe turn slowly and silently around that experience, and in the experience of allowing such an experience, we can only wonder what might appear in the spaces between the planets; in the spaces between the stars, in the spaces between the spaces as we could look out into the infinite space that the universe is. To be in this experience and then return from it can be an opportunity to look with fresh eyes, listen with fresh ears, experience some event, place, person or interaction and experience it as if for the first time, with nothing in the way of that freshness, that newness, that immediacy.

As you experience whatever is happening at any moment, there is no need to attend to the experience in any particular way; no need to attend to sensations that are of no concern; no need to attend to noises that are not relevant; but simply, relaxedly, effortlessly, allow the experience that is happening to be an experience that can in some way become a space for some new appreciating, some new recognition, some new opportunities to appear, as if from nowhere, not needing to have a use that is immediately apparent, and perhaps only after, or not even then, so that in some way, there can be more room, more space more opportunities to experience the wonder, the miraculous possibilities, the subtle and delightful experiences that are there, that we are, waiting to be experienced, whenever we take the time, create the space, allow the opportunity for whatever that might be to become visible, to appear out of nowhere, or somewhere, or wherever, so we have an opportunity to see them, to hear them, to experience them.

We can find ourselves sitting with a client, becoming absorbed in their experience, and allow any of our own thoughts, out own ideas, our own images, to drift into some silence, so not only can we disappear as an entity, not only can the client disappear as an entity, not only the floor, the walls, the ceiling, the furniture disappear into that same space, but there can then be an experience of total spaciousness and peace, which can then be experienced in any way that is of benefit, or value or use to the client, as they connect in their own way with their own resourcefulness – with the resourcefulness of the universe which surrounds them, and us, and contains an infinite variety of opportunities for learning, for developing, for experiencing.

And as with so many experiences, it's never necessary to fully or even partially recognise or understand the process of experiencing precisely what is needed to have that be come a part of our reality, because, after all, reality belongs to the universe, and it can be such a wondrous delight to explore some small aspect of what that might be, and how it might relate to us and to our future – individually and shared.

It is possible, then to have some awareness of this experience and have it exactly where it needs to be to be accessible, always with a sense of peace and fulfillment. And that is why I want to thank you for the opportunity to share this experience with you, and the less of me, the more of you can be available for your experience of what can be useful and relevant and satisfying for you, your future and your learning.

The Empathy Dilemma

We know intuitively and research confirms the importance of empathy. Empathy is defined in the Shorter Oxford Dictionary as "The power of projecting one's personality into, and so fully understanding, the object of contemplation." This contrasts with sympathy – "A (real or supposed) affinity between certain things, by virtue of which they are similarly or correspondingly affected by the same influence …"

We can only begin to work with another when we can see or sense something of the experience of that other and avoid some kind of internal hoping which leads to a projection of our perception and answer which has about the same likelihood of being useful as a lottery ticket.

If we set out to observe the client's experience, aware that we can never fully know another's experience, we can only wonder and be curious about what that might be. Without this, we run the risk of imposing our blind certainty and damaging the trust in the therapeutic relationship. By maintaining curiosity, we ensure the integrity of the individual client's experience and create rapport.

If we opt for sympathy rather than empathy, we run the risk of projecting our own experience and assuming that the client's experience is similar, and again we risk missing the individuality of the client, and generating an experience of disrespect in them.

Bateson said that the probe we stick into another human being also has an end that sticks into us, and if we project anything of ourselves into another, we will be influenced for better or worse.

Hence the dilemma.

Without empathy we are doomed to isolation and lack of contact with our client, and with it, we run the risk of being contaminated, or at least influenced by them.

This therapy dilemma directly parallels the broader human dilemma of intimacy. For us humans we need intimacy if we are to more than survive. We humans need intimacy like air, water and food. Without it we dry up and wither, like a neglected apple on a tree from last summer. And yet, the closeness of intimacy also brings risk – if we get close or allow another to get close, we may damage or be damaged, and our survival is at stake. So without intimacy, we might die, and if we allow intimacy, it might kill us.

Empathy in therapy brings a similar concern. If we project our personality or curiosity or some part of our awareness, attention, or focus onto or into our client, we must put awareness of our self, attention on our self, focus on yourself aside and for that time it is as if we cease to exist as a separate entity. This can be terrifying or ecstatic, but never dull or trivial.

This requirement to dissociate from ourselves and associate our attention on our client invites some learning. Firstly how to make the connection with the client, and then there is the return journey. If we don't learn to empathise or connect with our client, we are depriving them of the contact and the healing which is a part of any respectful human contact and any effective therapeutic intervention. If we don't learn to negotiate the reconnection or re-association with our self and away from the client, we will be left feeling disconnected from our self, and run the risk of carrying the mood and troubles of the client.

Firstly the learning how to empathise or wonder or project our curiosity into or at least towards the client:

An exercise I have found useful over the years to facilitate this experience is to sit with a colleague, facing them, and match their body position. Then if the other's breathing pattern and blinking pattern is matched, and any other movements, then there is a predictable alteration in the mood and experience of mutual connection with each reporting a sense of understanding and being understood. This coordination of action is defined as communication by Maturana. A mood of intimacy is frequently generated, and there are comments about blurring of boundaries, feeling close, sometimes accompanied by em-barrassment if this intimacy is a novel experience.

To facilitate empathy I have found that it is useful for me to suspend my own judgments, emotions, associations and interpretations as much as possible, and be open to those of the client. We can expected this to create rapport and contribute to the healing.

Another learning involves reconnecting with our own self again, after or perhaps at different stages during a therapy session. It can be helpful here to look away from the client, and begin to attend to some specific personal physical experiences – perhaps becoming aware of the sensations of our own feet on the floor, an awareness of the movement of air in and out of our nose or lungs – or to recall a personal experience of being centered, present to our own self – such as the experience of meditation or relaxation, or looking at a peaceful scene – and so have the experience, not just the idea, or reconnecting with our self again – our body, our preferred mood, our own personal experience.

If we have been with someone who has experienced some strong emotion that we don't like and don't want, a ritual activity can help – shaking our body to "shake the other person's experience" out of our bodily experience, or wash our hands. Sometimes a shower or a long soak in a hot bath seems required, and that is also worth noting and acting on as soon as is practical.

We can be alerted to the need to learn this if we are left tired, drained, burdened after a client has left or even while they are still with us – if it feels that we have done more than just been present to their problem, and actually taken it on.

It follows that to distinguish ownership of a problem is also a useful step. If we are left feeling down, overly optimistic, confused, or whatever – if this mood or experience seems foreign to us – can invite the question "Whose problem is this?" "Whose mood is this?" or "Whose experience is this?"

Because this is such a central concern for anyone wishing to be effective in their Counselling work, and still remain healthy and avoid burnout, it can be a useful practice to gain some facility with this process, and allow some practical learning over time by making recurrent opportunities to become familiar with the transition to and fro.

If we don't return the problem to its rightful owner, we run the risk of creating the consequences of any theft – having something that doesn't belong to us, leaving the owner without their possession, being caught, etc. – and if we have stolen the client's problem, however well intentionally, how can they begin to manage it and learn to deal with it if they no longer have it. On the other hand there are some problems that require something like a psychological or emotional or spiritual removal, but like any operator, we need to wear protective clothing, and clean up afterwards.

If we notice that we tend to recurrently associate with clients so we are left drained or disturbed, as well as learning to reconnect with our own experience, it can also be helpful to ask ourselves what we may be dissociating from in ourselves. Is there some personal distress or issue we may be avoiding? It's important to stress this as a possibility, an opportunity to be curious, not a definite indication.

One of the traps of any helping profession is just that – the helping. We may have entered our profession wanting to help – but what if the client doesn't want help, our doesn't want our help? If we blindly ignore our attachment to needing to help, we can generate frustration or resentment in ourselves, and boredom or disengagement in our clients. This can be a warning sign for us to examine out motives to ensure we don't use our clients for our own need of their dependency. De Shazer's distinctions of "customer," "complainant" and "visitor" can be soul saving and career saving here. Lao Tzu reminds us that "Knowing nothing needs to be done is the place we begin to move from."

These last two issues remind us of the value of supervision by a peer or a supervisor – someone we can usefully have conversations with to support and share and possibly formal therapeutic help since we are not immune from the human condition, however experienced we may be. A supportive, learning community can be nourishment for our soul.

After Trauma –
Healing The Mind Body And Soul

What does the solution orientation have to contribute?

Abstract

Much of our understanding and focus of assisting people who have suffered trauma has focused on thinking – ours and the clients' – and the body and soul have been neglected.

In this paper we can explore how the purposeful use of specific language forms can assist people who continue to suffer after trauma to reconnect with a more resourceful state. This can be achieved through active interventions involving their body, and inclusion of their soul or their fuller experience of themselves as a totality.

Traditionally, when we have attended to sufferers' thinking, and emotions, it is as a way of diagnosing their situation. In the solution orientation, questions are offered to help shift someone's thinking, emotions, and embodied experiences towards healing in a more direct manner, and can, on occasions, lead to a delightful relief for sufferer and clinician.

In this paper, these questions will be explored, and cases offered to illustrate the approach.

Viktor Frankl wrote of a widower who was devastated by the death of his wife of many years. He could not find any reason to go on living without his life-long soul mate. Frankl asked him if he would rather that he died first, since one of them had to, so that his wife would have to go through this?

His despair dissolved and he was able to leave peacefully, even gratefully. How was this possible? There had been no change in his circumstances, no insight into his dilemma, no outpouring of repressed emotions, and yet the impasse was able to be resolved totally.

When a client comes to us for help with a trauma, they usually bring a mind set that their circumstances need to change. History needs to be re-written, the incident needs to be erased so that they will then be OK. This is beyond the therapeutic skills of most of us mere mortal therapists.

Other times a client may have some recognition that the traumatic events can't be undone, and yet that recognition is insufficient for them to let it go. It is as if the trauma is stuck in their body and reason alone is insufficient to shift it.

A core issue here is the human condition. We humans have the blessings and limitations of being linguistic beings. We live in language, and after Maturana we can say we are created as individual identities in language. It is this linguistic aspect that is the source of our suffering and also the way out of the same suffering.

A colleague told me that he was assisting a client to come to terms with her trauma, and was wanting her to see the difference between pain as a suffering. He explained to her that we experience pain is a result of the stimulation of nerve endings, whereas suffering is a function of what meaning we attach to the painful sensations. She couldn't get it until later that day, she approached her dog which was resting in the shade of a tree recuperating from a recently broken leg. As she began to pat the dog, it bit her, and she reported that at that moment she suddenly recognised that the dog had the pain, and she had the suffering.

It is this capacity for suffering that transcends rationality and concerns of the mind. This is the human soul at work. No amount of reasoning will convince a client until we address their soul – their individual way of being that is at the core of who they are. That part of us that is like a dog with a bone when where the bone goes, the dog goes. Our soul is our "bone," and if we try and remove a bone, we are likely to increase everyone's suffering in the struggle that will inevitably be created.

I am increasingly grateful for Milton Erickson's contribution here. Two of his comments seem particularly relevant - *"Because each person is an individual, we need to tailor our approach to meet the individual's needs rather than tailor the person to fit some Procrustean bed of psychological theory"… and …"To think that there can be one psychological theory that would fit every individual of both sexes, of all ages, all races and religions, in all circumstances is ridiculous."*

I like his implied invitation for us to look beyond the external circumstances that a client brings to us, beyond any diagnostic label, and focus instead on the person, their experience, and their individual response which is the source of their suffering and the source of the nascent solution. By shifting the focus from and inquiry into what's wrong, and towards what might be missing for each individual client is not a trivial matter. It may be worth the existential discomfort of letting go of *our* need for certainty, of us not knowing what's best for the client, and daring to look, with the client, for what will be most helpful to them.

My medical training had me learn to gather information to make a diagnosis to create a treatment plan and then begin to implement it. While this approach will be useful or even necessary in dealing with some problems, physically based ones particularly, there is another approach which is worth exploring.

If we begin with the question of what's missing for this individual client, we can begin to explore with them what resource they may have lost track of. If we can assist them to reconnect with that experience, they may then be ready to deal with their dilemma and even solve it.

Mind Matters – A Therapeutic Use Of Language
For too long we have relegated language to a secondary role of merely describing how things are. Language is finally re-

emerging and being recognised as an active generator of future experiences.

A patient in a psychiatric hospital was in an art class, and the teacher was impressed with the quality of the paintings. She said to him "You're an artist." This was news to him. He thought he was a psychiatric patient! He was able to leave the hospital and earn a living painting and making furniture. Many people view his work as strange, but he is a functioning member of society, living independently, and no longer requiring psychiatric care. His change happened in language. When the art teacher said he was an artist, a whole new future was created in that moment, and he was able to live into THAT future rather than the one he had been anticipating.

We can begin with the assumption, and it can only be an assumption, that each client has what they need to move on in their life, and that they are stuck because they have lost track of that capacity. We can then begin to explore, with them, what that experience may be. For someone who has a nagging incompleteness around the event it might be remembering the event. Others who are haunted by flashbacks might rather forget the trauma or at least have it more in the background as part of their total experience. Obviously there will be many clients who will be between these two extremes.

A woman was driving to work, and lost control of her car as it went round a bend in the road. The car rolled over several times, and although she stepped out of the car unhurt, every time she thought of driving, memories of the car spinning and emotions of fear – fear that she was about to die – came flooding into her mind. She said, almost as a throw away line "I wish I could get the accident right out of my mind. I just want to forget it" but thought that would not be possible. I asked her about how she had dealt with other crises in her life, and she said that after some time she always came to a decision, and told herself that enough is enough, and then she could move on. She then stated that perhaps it was time for her to do that with the accident, and was able to get into her car and drive, with minimal and decreasing discomfort.

I like to begin by asking a client what they like to do. Asking about likes can be a delightful way of lightening the mood which can be therapeutic in itself. Speaking about likes also helps to evoke a resourcefulness state since we only like activities that we feel adequately resourceful about. Bringing lightness and resourceful-ness into the conversation can be such a delightful relief for all. It is as if there is more of the client in the room, more of them available to deal with their situation.

A bank teller loved his garden, and his roses in particular. He had a wide variety and was proud of his garden, which was widely admired. He was delighted to tell me about the importance of watering the plants without overdoing it, pruning any dead blooms and unwanted branches. He considered himself something of a self taught expert. He wanted help with his sleeping since his bank had been held up by an armed robber. He was waking with nightmares reliving the robbery, and creating additional scenes of horror imagining what might have happened. I asked him how he might use his gardening skill to help his situation, and after being surprised, he began to ponder which thoughts could be pruned, which fed, which ignored, and then told me that he would be OK. Two weeks later he was sleeping well, and told me that he was enjoying reading gardening books just before he went to sleep, and that he knew that this was helping. His skills as a gardener could be transplanted to the problem area and simply grafted on so that he could be an active participant in his own healing.

I then like to ask about what beneficial changes have already begun, and by exploring these there can be an opportunity to acknowledge that change has begun, and then by clarifying how the client has achieved these changes, however small, the possibility of extending them and amplifying them appears for the first time. I have been impressed with the delight apparent on the face of such a client when they discover that the process that they brought to us has already begun, and they began it! Our work together, then, is merely to keep the momentum up and provide support along the way.

Asking about how they will be different when the trauma is resolved can assist to create the possibility of a resolution. This recognition can be such a relief for a client stuck in a mind set of having to "learn to live with it." De Shazer's miracle question can also move the conversation in a useful direction. *"If when you go to sleep tonight the problem were to disappear, what would be different when you woke up in the morning?"* Speaking the possibility can feel like a miracle to someone stuck in the mire of resignation and despair.

A man was suicidal after being made redundant at work. He was having trouble applying for other jobs, and couldn't see the point in it all. I asked him what would be different if a miracle happened and all his problems were solved. His mood lifted obviously, and he said that he would have a job again. When I asked him about how that would feel, he reported that he would feel worthwhile, knowing that he could support his family who were so important to him. I commented on how different he looked even talking about the possibility, and he recognised that change in mood also. He was then able to recognise that he had all he needed to continue, and he had always wanted to have his own business instead of working for someone else, and he stated at that moment, that he had enough money put aside to pay a deposit on a truck and he could begin his own taxi trucking enterprise. He left optimistic, and started his business which thrived.

Moods And Emotions

Emotions have been traditionally seen as indicators of areas for exploration, like a water diviner's rod hinting at where to dig for water. Following Maturana, we can see that emotions, like language, are closely related to action, and he defines them as predispositions for action. In different emotions, we are differently predisposed to take different actions. After a trauma we expect some sort of sadness, which predisposes us to deal with the loss, and fear, which predisposes us to be concerned about the future continuing as a recycling of the past.

We can identify these emotions, allow for a fuller expression of them, but we can do more than that. We can also explore, with the individual, what emotions they might prefer or find more useful. Emotions such as acceptance, peace, security or hopefulness might then become a useful direction or orientation. We can speak with such an individual and ask them how they have felt when they have experienced peace, or whatever desirable emotion they want, in the past, how they might recognise such an experience if it were to happen sometime in the near future, or if they may even already be beginning to have at least a hint of that even as we are speaking together.

A Vietnam vet was wracked with guilt after his war experiences and shame that so much of what had happened was hidden. He felt resentment that instead of being treated like a hero when he returned home, he was vilified. He was agitated, and flew into a rage with very little provoking. When I asked him how he would rather feel, he wanted to find a way of forgiving himself for his actions so he would be less resentful of the situation he had been forced into. I asked him how he "did" guilt. If I wanted to feel guilt the way he did, what would I need to do? He was able to describe precisely how he produced the guilt, and he was bemused to hear what he was saying. He was even more bemused when he heard himself giving me clear instructions about how I might forgive myself like he had already forgiven himself for so many mistakes in his past. As he described the actions he had taken to forgive himself previously, he was reminding himself of how he could forgive himself in this situation. He was very relieved, and over the following year made steady progress in reclaiming his fuller expression of himself.

By giving clients a more direct access to their solution emotions, the process can move more respectfully, and more humanly forward with less suffering all round.

The Body's Contribution

Some traumas and their accompanying emotions seem to take up residence in the body, and like "The Alien," take it over and seem reluctant to let go of it. An emotion of fear or sadness can settle in to become a pervasive background mood. We see this in clients with stooped shoulders, eyes looking at the floor, flat facial muscles. Such a body won't allow solutions. Traditionally, we have looked to the body as evidence that some useful change after it has happened, but we can also foster the likelihood of such a change by encouraging a body position which will allow for the desired outcome to be more likely.

To ask a client to stand, shoulders erect, eyes looking straight ahead, or even a little higher does more than change the body position, it changes what they see, who the person is, what they can experience, what is possible for them. Asking such a client to place their open hands in front of them, palms upwards can be a delightful opening for trust to have an opportunity to present itself for learning.

A woman in her 30s was having panic attacks after the traumatic delivery of her second child several years previously. She said that she thought her labour was never going to end and that she knew she was going to die. She thought that the drugs she had been given for her pain may have confused her and added to the feeling of overwhelming fear that at any moment something terrible was going to happen. I asked her how she would rather be, and she readily discovered that she would rather be more confident. When I asked her to show my how her body would be if she were more confident, and she stood up, shoulders back, a peaceful look on her face and said "Like this!" I recommended that she spend a little time getting reacquainted with this "confident body" and encouraged her to take her own time relearning this fully. This experience was a turning point for her. It was as if her body was given an opportunity to remind her of the experience so she could reconnect with it more regularly. She continued to be somewhat edgy for several weeks, but there was no recurrence of her panic, and the edginess subsided gradually over the next few months.

Healing The Soul

Garfield and Bergin (1994) claim that after client factors, the therapeutic relationship accounts for the greatest contribution to a client's healing – double that of technique, whichever that may be. We humans are relating beings, and as Maturana says "The patient begins to get better when the doctor accepts the call." The relationship is such a powerful influence, and forms the context for any therapeutic intervention to take effect.

We live in an age of technology, with all the failed promises that came with it. We were promised easier work, a paperless office, time savings. No-one can doubt the benefits of computers, but like the advent of the gas stove, a greater range of more nutritious meals resulted, but no saving of money, effort, or time. Computers have created new opportunities for humans, email and the internet being the most enriching, but I'm sure

I'm not the only one who spends hours every week backing up, installing upgrades, checking for viruses ... the list continues.

One down side of the technological turn has been the disconnection it can bring. People spend time chatting on the computer without any physical connection. How many hours do people, adults and children, spend looking at TV? There's no interaction, only passive entertainment. The contact that a face to face conversation offers is becoming a rarity, and we are suffering as a result.

Medicine has not been immune from this ill. GPs are finding difficulty in doing more than asking a few questions, writing a script, ordering a pathology test or scan, or referring on to a specialist. The old fashioned family doctor is a romantic memory from a past era, to everyone's loss.

It is a tragedy that there doesn't seem to be enough time for patients and doctors to have a human conversation, and it is my opinion that this is the cause of the soul going out of medicine. There are some signs of rehabilitation happening, and I hope it's not too late.

We know as human beings how beneficial it is to speak with someone we trust, to share a burden, to explore an idea, to be together in a conference such as this. It is my experience that when I leave a conference, I have gained more than information and skills. My soul has been nourished. My spirit lifted, and I'm more fully ready to work and learn.

We know this, and yet technology has seduced us from what we know to be humanly relevant and healing.

When we offer ourselves to a client in a mood of respect, acceptance – of love – healing can begin at the level of the soul. We have all had the experience of being with a client and applying some technique. The mechanistic approach dehumanises the client and us. We have also had the experience of being genuinely present with a client, in the mystery of their experience, in the wonder of their exploring, in the vulnerable reaching out however tenuously towards their own future – a future which allows their mind to rest, their mood to become peaceful, their body to settle, and their soul to dance and breathe.

About The Author

Robert McNeilly was in general medical practice for 10 years, conducted a private hypnotherapy practice for 30 years, and after meeting Milton H Erickson in USA, began teaching diploma courses in Counselling and hypnosis with a solution orientation to interested health workers nationally and internationally.

He has authored 2 books - "Healing with Words" with Jenny Brown and "Healing the Whole Person" published by Wiley, recently republished as "Doing Change - conversations for moving on" by St Luke's Innovative Resources. He has also published a number of eBooks with Amazon Kindle.

Robert B McNeilly MBBS
Director, The Centre of Effective Therapy
Co-director, The Milton H Erickson Institute of Tasmania
191 Campbell Street
Hobart TAS 7000
Australia

email rob@cet.net.au
www.cet.net.au
robmcneilly.com